Don Moll

Bringing together qualifications as an outstanding teacher and philosopher in what he calls "a personal book," **Frederick Ferré** is equally at home in the lay and academic worlds. Dr. Ferré is Charles A. Dana Professor of Philosophy at Dickinson College and the author of several books, including **Language, Logic, and God.**

D1473985

SHAPING THE FUTURE

SHAPING
THE FUTURE

Resources for the Post-Modern World

1817

Frederick Ferré

HARPER & ROW, PUBLISHERS
New York, Hagerstown, San Francisco, London

ACKNOWLEDGMENTS

Grateful acknowledgment is made to the following for permission to reprint selections included in this book:

DOUBLEDAY AND COMPANY for quotes from *The Making of a Counter-Culture,* by Theodore Rozak. Copyright © 1968–69 by Theodore Rozak. Also for quotes from *The Coming of the Golden Age,* by Gunther S. Stent Copyright © 1969 by Gunther S. Stent. Reprinted with permission of Doubleday and Company.

ALFRED A. KNOPF, INC. for excerpts from *The Closing Circle: Nature, Man and Technology,* by Barry Commoner. Copyright © 1971 by Barry Commoner. Reprinted by permission of Alfred A. Knopf, Inc. Portions of the book originally

FIRST EDITION

Designed by Patricia Dunbar

Library of Congress Cataloging in Publication Data

CB
428
·F48
1976

Ferré, Frederick.
  Shaping the future.
  Includes index.
  1. Civilization, Modern—1950–
2. Civilization—Philosophy. 3. Christianity—
Philosophy. 4. Technology and civilization.
I. Title.
CB428.F48 1976   909.82   75–36755
ISBN 0–06–062371–3

76 77 78 79 10 9 8 7 6 5 4 3 2 1

For Kammie,
our daughter,

whose values will help
to shape the future world

appeared in the New Yorker. Also for excerpts from *Beyond Freedom and Dignity*, by B. F. Skinner. Copyright © 1971 Alfred A. Knopf, Inc. and also for excerpts from *Chance and Necessity*, by Jacques Monod, translated by Austryn Wainhouse. Copyright © 1971 Alfred A. Knopf, Inc. and also *The Technological Society*, by Jacques Ellul, translated by John Wilkinson. Copyright © 1964 by Alfred A. Knopf, Inc. Reprinted by permission of Alfred A. Knopf, Inc.

E. P. DUTTON & COMPANY, INC. for quotations from *Mankind at the Turning Point: The Second Report to the Club of Rome,* by Mihajlo Mesarovic and Eduard Pestel. Copyright © 1974 by Mihajlo Mesarovic and Eduard Pestel. Reprinted by permission of the publishers, E. P. Dutton & Company, Inc.

MACMILLAN PUBLISHING COMPANY, INC. for quotations from *Science and the Modern World,* by A. N. Whitehead. Copyright © 1925 by Macmillan Publishing Company, Inc. Copyright renewed 1953 by Evelyn Whitehead.

HAROLD K. SCHILLING for quotation from his book *The New Consciousness in Science and Religion.* Copyright © 1973 United Church Press. Reprinted with permission from Harold K. Schilling.

UNIVERSE BOOKS for quotations from *The Limits to Growth: A Report for THE CLUB OF ROME'S Project on the Predicament of Mankind,* by Donella H. Meadows, Jørgen Randers, William W. Behrens III. A Potomac Associates book published by Universe Books, New York, 1972. Graphics by Potomac Associates.

CONTENTS

PREFACE

This book is the product of many concerns and interests—
professional and personal—that have come together for me in
a compelling way only recently. Readers who are acquainted
with my work in the philosophy of religion will recognize
some familiar themes, here put to work for more general
purposes. Similarly, my work in the history and philosophy of
science over the past decade or more has woven itself into the
pages that follow. I am especially grateful to Thomas S. Kuhn
for his hospitality and inspiration at Princeton during my
sabbatical year, 1969–1970.

Both of these interests have merged, for me, at the threshold
of what might be called the philosophy of nature and culture,
or environmental-social philosophy. Since 1969 I have
increasingly engaged myself with such matters, for which I
have largely to thank Philip N. Joranson and his now
disbanded Faith-Man-Nature Group, whose invitation to
participate at an Airlie House conference gave my own
consciousness a tremendous push. The FMN group was

devoted to bringing natural scientists, conservationists, forestry experts, and the like face to face with theologians and philosophers in order to stimulate thinking that is long-term, fundamental, comprehensive, and responsible about the enormous challenges facing humanity in developing radically reformed policies toward the earth and each other.

Another major influence in recent years has been from my Dickinson College colleague, Priscilla Laws, who has planned and taught with me a stimulating and ever-varied course in environmental studies. Professor Laws, a physicist, and I have attempted to deal with the interaction of physical fact and cultural value on the ecosystem. We have sometimes worked historically, sometimes crossculturally, always with contemporary questions in mind; we have from time to time been fruitfully joined by colleagues in anthropology, political science, economics, biology, physics, and religion; and we have been helped by having eager and able students to work with us in our quest for positive answers to the impending crisis of our modern civilization.

As my ideas on the relationship between spiritual vision, nature, and society were developing during the early 1970s, I was fortunate to have a band of colleagues, the Science-Theology Group (composed of scientists, theologians, and philosophers meeting twice annually for discussion), with whom I could converse freely and from whom I could receive first-rate criticisms and stimulation. My most sincere gratitude is given, therefore, to Harold K. Schilling (physics, Pennsylvania State University), inspirer of the group, and to my fellow active members, Ian Barbour (religion and physics, Carleton College), the late George Bradley (physics, Western Michigan University), Herman Carr (physics, Rutgers University), John Compton (philosophy, Vanderbilt University), Harmon Holcomb (philosophy, University of Rochester), John Ollom (physics, Drew University), William Pollard (physics, Oak Ridge Associated Universities), Roger Shinn (social ethics, Union Theological Seminary), Huston Smith (philosophy, Syracuse University), Henry Torrey (physics, Rutgers

University), Charles West (theology, Princeton Theological Seminary), and the late Daniel Day Williams (theology, Union Theological Seminary). In March, 1975, a session of our meeting at Pennsylvania State University was devoted to a sustained discussion, from which my revisions and expansions of the five "core" chapters of this book benefited greatly.

The immediate occasion for the writing of those five initial chapters was an invitation to give a week's series of lectures at Chautauqua, New York, in August of 1974. President Oscar Remick of the Chautauqua Institution suggested that the centennial season at Chautauqua was to be spent looking ahead as well as back, informing me that the overall theme for the religion lectures would be the "Future of Christianity in the Post-Modern World." I am grateful both for the delightful week at Chautauqua—an incomparable place—and for the challenge provided by the theme. Chapters 1, 2, 4, 5, and 6, are based on the 1974 Chautauqua lectures, though each has been more or less revised. Most transformed of all is chapter 6, which originally devoted exclusive attention to Christianity (in response to the Chautauqua theme) but now has been generalized in keeping with my own pluralistic religious stance to introduce what I call Polymythic Organicism.

The application of this philosophicoreligious position to religion, education, politics, and economics in our culture required three new chapters, 7, 8, and 9, comprising part three. These were written a year after my lectures at Chautauqua at my summer residence in New Hampshire.

The other new chapter, chapter 3, is the revised version of a lecture prepared for presentation before a joint colloquium sponsored by the nuclear engineering and chemical engineering departments at Purdue University in February 1975, and another form of the same lecture presented to a biology department seminar at Wabash College in April 1975. I am grateful to Professor Paul Lykoudis, head of the nuclear engineering department at Purdue, for his original invitation and his subsequent criticisms.

Another pleasant and useful invitation came from Dennis

and Donella Meadows, at Dartmouth College, to visit not only
in the summer of 1974, while the Chautauqua lectures were in
preparation, but also in 1975 when this book was nearing
completion in its present form. On the second visit I was
asked to lead a seminar for the whole Meadows team, which
gave me an opportunity both to present my point of view to
the group whose systems analyses lie behind the *Limits to
Growth* debate, and to receive immediate and sustained
reaction from that vital team of variegated experts. It was an
exciting and wholly positive occasion for which I remain in
their debt.

The year between the original writing of the Chautauqua
lectures and the final version of the book I spent happily at
Purdue University as Eli Lilly Visiting Professor of Science,
Theology, and Human Values. It was an important year in all
respects. I was able to devote myself full-time to integrative
teaching in the areas of my interest, and, best of all, was able
to receive the stimulus of new colleagues from a variety of
disciplines. Professor Richard Grabau, head of the philosophy
department and chairman of the Lilly Committee that brought
me to Purdue and nurtured me there, deserves extraordinary
thanks. Special gratitude, also, is due to the colleagues who
gathered to discuss my "Chatauqua chapters" on Thursday
noons during the year. I cannot name them all, but the
comments and criticisms from Professors Joseph Haberer
(political science), David Moore (statistics), Gary J. Quinn
(theology, Notre Dame), Ronald Barile (chemical engineering),
and Leo Haigerty (campus ministry) were especially important
to my revisions.

I wish I had been able to make really adequate use of their
thoughtful advice, but I have done what I can. This book has
been written, from initial Chautauqua lectures to final
submission of manuscript, during a leave of absence that has
put me out of reach of nearly all my books and notes. This
has been frustrating, at times, but the main effect has been
liberating. I have no illusions of having written a scholar's

book for fellow scholars. It is a personal book for other persons.

My other books may have been better defended and documented, but this book has grown out of an altered setting and a different need. I am urgently concerned about our current historical condition and have written from the heart as well as from the head. Some of my fellow philosophers, if they read this, may wonder whether it is philosophy at all. I am not certain that it is. It is manifestly not technical philosophy. Many of my assertions are underdefended and imperfectly qualified. But Wittgenstein held that philosophy is a way of finding one's way about; and this, in the context of our current ecohistorical confusions, is what I am attempting to do here. Sometimes, I think, it is right to do so even if it makes one vulnerable to scholarly barbs from those who take care always to be well armored.

No one today, however, ought to feel completely secure. We are all vulnerable to the gigantic tides of history that are sweeping over the world, calling into radical question the values and structures of the modern world and thrusting us, willy-nilly, toward a post-modern era.

A word is needed on my use of the terms *modern* and *post-modern.* I realize that one correct and common use of the word *modern* is simply to refer to whatever is current at the time. This is a temporal pointing, or indexical, use of the term. On this use, whatever is happening *now* (another indexical word) is ipso facto *modern.* And on this use it simply does not make sense to speak of *post-modern* in the way that I do in this book. It would be like referring to *post-now* furniture or the like—not very illuminating.

But there is another sense of *modern* that I prefer for the purposes of historical reflection and social criticism. In this other sense, *modern* is not merely an indexical sign, as empty of descriptive content as *here* or *now,* but is rather a designative term with certain general descriptive properties attached. Those properties are the fundamental marks of what we sometimes call *modernization* or *modernity*. On this usage, it is possible for persons to be living "now" but to eschew "modern" ways. The Amish, we can properly say, have deliberately preferred not to join the modern world, although they live simultaneously with it. Likewise, some nations (and farmhouses) are becoming "modernized," for better or for worse.

In this descriptive use of the term *modern,* it is possible to think of the general set of properties that define *modernity* as having a beginning, a history, and even an ending. What would follow the "modern," then, would be the "post-modern." I do not suppose that this will be the name that post-modernity gives to its culture (nor, perhaps, will *modern* be the label finally given to our historical era), but for the time being we need some open phrase to name what comes after the characteristically modern world we know so well. It is an evidence of the powerful grip of familiar modern consciousness, indeed, that our language itself seems to resist the possibility of modernity ever being supplanted.

One whose mind is already probing for the post-modern world is my friend, colleague, and summer neighbor, Dr. Peter Baldwin, with whom I have discussed these chapters in various drafts after writing and sharing them on our lovely Pancake Hill. To Peter, post-modern psychologist; to Thomas Wagner, administrative assistant for Senator Adlai Stevenson III and man of political affairs; to their insightful wives Carolyn and Judy; to kind and critical visitors to the hill, Samuel Magill, Barbara Meister, and Lindi Martin, all educators; to Bernard J. Pond, Newell S. Booth, Jr., and M. David Stein, friendly critics; and to my wife, Marie, I owe much in encouragement and refinement. Rural nature offered its inspiration as I wrote this mainly out-of-doors; friends and loved ones have provided their support—I am deeply in their debt.

Frederick Ferré
Hiroshima Day, 1975

Pancake Hill
Lower Gilmanton, N.H.

I
THE ENDING OF THE
MODERN WORLD

1. MYTHIC MATRIX

The most important fact about our current historical situation is hard to accept: that our modern world is in its last days (or already largely ended) and that we are—ready or not, like it or not—entering a turbulent period of transition to a very different world of post-modernity.

This fact, accepted or not, is occasioning deep spiritual distress, unfocused and shallow though it may presently be. Convulsive shifts are occurring deep in the bedrock of our cultural assumptions. Hitherto mainly unquestioned expectations of continuous growth, hitherto mainly unchallenged virtues of technical expertise, hitherto mainly unexamined images of the future as endless variations on the familiar themes of modernity itself—all have come under scrutiny and have been found wanting.

Much of our current distress springs from sheer bewilderment in the face of collapsing certitudes; much arises from fear of the crumbling of material affluence, on which life's meaning has been too firmly anchored. Our urgent need is for philosophic perspective broad enough, and for religious

1

resources strong enough to cope with change on an order of
magnitude that occurs seldom in human history.

Civilizations, we know, do sometimes come to an end. The
world of classical Greece, the world of imperial Rome, the
medieval world, have all flourished and declined and been
replaced. Our modern world, we must remember, is no less
mortal. When changes go deep enough there is good point in
speaking of worlds coming to an end and new worlds being
born. Ours is one such time in history, and our destiny is to
live at the crossroads leading to whatever post-modern world
the present may produce.

I

The modern world began in the seventeenth century, rising,
with the rise of modern science, out of the very different
worlds of Renaissance humanism and, before that, of the
medieval civilization. Modernity blossomed in the eighteenth
century with the industrial revolution; it gathered momentum
and geographical extent through conquest and by imitation in
the nineteenth century; it came to its climax in the twentieth
century, though shaken by two great internal wars—involving
newly modernized Japan as well as earlier modernized
European powers—and is now dangerously balanced on
nuclear stalemate between modernized Russia and modernized
America, the two continental powers to the east and west,
respectively, of mother Europe where modernity began.

This modern world is ending now. Its very climax in the
mid-twentieth century reveals the impossibility of its indefinite
continuation.

One clear and, alas, still entirely too likely ending for the
modern world would be by war, with modernity's own dread
weapons turned against itself. How easy it would be to slip off
the trembling poised point of mutual deterrence—especially as
partially modernized nations like India or Egypt overload the
already groaning political gyroscopes of the great powers with
new complexities and sudden lurches! But how difficult—no,

impossible—it would be to rebuild a modern civilization out of the radioactive rubble of nuclear world war! After nuclear holocaust a modern world would never reappear: not because all humanity would necessarily be destroyed (though the survivors would undoubtedly be deeply changed, ipso facto post-modern humans), but rather because the immensely complex and vulnerable fabric of high modern technological society, once thoroughly torn, would be infinitely more difficult to repair than it was to weave in the first place.

The earth is no longer, and never will be again, naïvely bountiful, after three hundred years of avid exploitation by the ever-expansive appetites of the modern world. Much of the easily mined copper and other essentials for high technology, most of the easily extracted oil and other energy sources required for recognizably modern living—these have been used up already in the centuries-long process of building the world we now inhabit. With the vast technological investments of that world atomized, the elaborate methods now needed to find and extract the essential resources for a modern society would be denied to the survivors even if, after the unthinkable trauma of nuclear war, such survivors wanted to return to the ways of their forebears and reconstruct a modern-style world. It looks as though one modern technological society is the maximum that this planet (perhaps any planet) can allow to arise; once this complex phenomenon, which must provide the sophisticated technological means for its own growth and feeding, is destroyed or severely wounded, we should not expect a second, ever again, upon the depleted earth.

War, however, may not be inevitable. *Perhaps* Kenneth Boulding is right in arguing that the practice of warfare can be unlearned—as it must be if we are to avoid such a doom— and new peaceful practices learned in time. "The abolition of war," he says, ". . . requires a twofold learning process, one where the values and behavior states themselves change toward longsightedness, toward accurate reality testing of power systems, and toward a value system that lays stress on the welfare of all humanity. The other is a learning process whereby we develop the institutions of third-party intervention on a world scale."[1]

If humanity should have the good fortune and the good sense to learn such important lessons, after a five-thousand year habit of organized warfare, we would indeed be at a most important junction in human history. Perhaps we are. Let us fervently hope—and actively work—that this may be the case! But all the more reason—if we are at such a great transition point in the human story on this planet—to foresee the inevitable end of the modern world. Such anticipations arise not merely because the end of warfare would pose such a vivid contrast to the warring history of modernity, though it would certainly do so, but more importantly because the escape from the end by war would allow the modern world to work out to their natural limits some of the dynamics that have been essential to modernity itself from its beginning. I refer, of course, to the impossible curves of exponential growth that have characterized the modern world and only now, at the climax and near the end, show themselves so startlingly as nemesis.

One such curve is population. A characteristic of modernity, from its early origins in Europe to its current impact on India and all other parts of the world, has been the reduction of the death rate and the bounding upwards of population. The agricultural revolution of early modern times, then the industrial revolution, now the "Green Revolution," have tended to support the steady increase of populations. But people do not grow merely additively, by arithmetic progression; they grow, as Malthus saw long ago, by multiplication or geometrically. Like money in a bank at compound interest, where money that is earned (and left) itself starts earning, so people that are born (and live) themselves produce more people. At first the growth appears well under control, but a characteristic of geometric growth is the suddenness with which the growth curve rises toward the end.

Anything growing at a geometric rate has its own characteristic doubling time (a bank account growing at 7 percent compounded interest, for example, doubles approximately every ten years), and anything that doubles regularly has this surprising exponential upshoot characteristic. The authors of *The Limits to Growth* illustrate it well:

> There is an old Persian legend about a clever courtier who presented a beautiful chessboard to his king and requested that the king give him in return 1 grain of rice for the first square on the board, 2 grains for the second square, 4 grains for the third and so forth. The king readily agreed and ordered rice to be brought from his stores. The fourth square of the chessboard required eight grains, the tenth square took 512 grains, the fifteenth required 16,384, and the twenty-first square gave the courtier more than a million grains of rice. By the fortieth square a million million rice grains had to be brought from the storerooms. The king's entire rice supply was exhausted long before he reached the sixty-fourth square.[2]

I attempted to follow this story on my electronic desk calculator, but my machine, which can display up to 99,999,999, overloaded after only twenty-six doublings! Exponential increase begins with deceptive innocence; but inevitably it zooms out of sight.

We are now at the alarming end of this characteristic mathematical curve with regard to world population. The prospects of disastrously overloading the world system—analogous to the sudden overloading of my electric calculator —are suddenly very vivid. A few more doublings, only, and social collapse on a scale unprecedented in the whole of human history awaits large portions of humanity. Since the rate of doubling in some areas has itself been increasing, people alive today will witness the cataclysmic consequences in famine, chaos, and plague that will surely sweep the world unless something is done immediately to halt the process of exponential population increase.

There are those who doubt that the population problems of

the semimodernized nations need necessarily threaten the fully modernized areas of the world. The "let them starve" theory purports to trade on realism despite its moral callousness. It is true that most fully modernized nations seem to have overcome the worst aspects of population growth through voluntary restraints on reproduction rates. It is false, however, to imagine these momentarily fortunate nations as secure in their own "lifeboats."[3] The proliferation of nuclear capability among modernizing nations shows how problems of war may someday be linked to problems of population, as nations driven sufficiently desperate by starvation force attention to their need. The balance of terror holds little restraint for governments who could be facing as many millions of deaths from famine and plague as from war. We are truly the inhabitants of one world.

Population dynamics alone could guarantee the end, then, of the modern world as we have known it. But other essential features of our world show precisely the same fatal exponential characteristics and will therefore inevitably overload the finite planetary system no matter how bountiful our planet or how clever our technological devices. The reason is clear: namely, that exponential growth inevitably bumps against *any* limit, however distant or generous, since the doubling process itself is inherently open-ended. One might debate just how distant and generous the earth's limits are in various dimensions that are characteristic of our modern world:[4] the dimension of the nonrenewable natural resources we need to manufacture our goods and to power our industries; the dimension of the earth's capacity to absorb the pollution generated by our modern way of life; the dimension of the earth's capacity to produce more food for more people without finally poisoning the soil and ecosphere beyond recovery. One might debate these and other limits on matters of detailed estimates of how soon our characteristically modern exponential curves meet their implacable end, but that there *are* limits—that the earth is finite and not infinite—this is not open to reasonable doubt. Thus since the modern world's demands for energy, for foodstuffs, and for manufactured goods, as well as the modern world's output of people and pollution, are all firmly on exponential curves, the modern world—if it escapes ending by war—will not escape ending.

Either the ending will be involuntary and tragic, through the dooms of starvation and disease, or through widespread pollution catastrophe, or through economic collapse due to exhaustion of nonrenewable resources; or the ending will be voluntary and, as I have said earlier, merely horrendously difficult. The difficulty will be in parting with characteristics that have been the familiar defining marks of the modern world: progressivism will need to be given up for stability, growth will need to give way to steady-state or even shrinking expectations, exploitation of nature will need to be replaced by balancing with nature.

The old order of the past three centuries is ending. The new, post-modern world has not emerged. These therefore are times of great transition in which all our resources, spiritual and intellectual no less than material, need full deployment to meet the challenges of our future and our present.

What are these spiritual resources? How do they function—for good or ill—in this transition time? The purpose of this book, given the great premise of change I have now sketched, is to examine our situation in philosophical and religious terms. In chapters 2 and 3, I shall dig for the religious roots of modern consciousness—the consciousness that germinated at the start of modern times and blossomed into the modern world that is now fatefully ending. Then in part 2, I shall examine possible post-modern alternatives, both traditional and new. Finally, in part 3, I shall offer the outlines of a strategy for living creatively through this painful transition to the next age.

There is no point in trying to *predict* what the successor age with its characteristic consciousness will be like. Events will play too great a part in shaping it. What would human consciousness be like in a post-modern age brought about by nuclear holocaust? How would it be like (or different from) human consciousness set within a desperately overcrowded world or one set in a period of planetary ecological collapse? How would these "doom models" compare with human consciousness in a post-modern world that has renounced the dynamics of material growth and the obsession with consumption—successfully managing both its social conflicts and its relations with the natural environment? No one can say for sure what the next age will be like, except that it will be different in basic ways from the modern, and that the characteristic human consciousness of the post-modern world will be correspondingly different from the dominant consciousness—how we value, perceive, feel, and believe—that we mainly share today.

Still, while it is futile to predict future consciousness, it is not unreasonable to hope to influence current consciousness. And since this is a time of transition in which emerging values, perceptions, feelings and beliefs will have much to do with shaping current decisions giving rise to the future events that will in turn reciprocally influence future consciousness, we stand at a point of potentially significant leverage.

II

What remains for this chapter is the laying out of some of the conceptual tools needed for our task. I shall try to avoid most technicalities in this book, but settling on certain common concepts will be useful before we proceed any farther.[5]

In the first place I am convinced that if we are to deal with the religious foundations of great historical movements we had better take a broad view of religion. Any conception of religion that limits our view to the recognized institutionalized religions—Christianity, Judaism, Islam and the rest—will leave out of account religious phenomena of the utmost importance. The recognized religions (ideally) function for their adherents as all religions do—providing a focus for worship, a vision of reality, a basis in shared values and perceptions for community, and a sense of personal significance—indeed, they provide what we must recognize as paradigm cases of what it means to perform fundamental religious functions. But these functions are also performed by other spiritually powerful agencies—for example Communism in certain circumstances, or Nazism for many under Hitler, or Nationalism for many today—which thereby become the real functional religions for their adherents, even though those adherents may continue to give lip service to one of the institutional religions in their society.

Religious leaders of the latter variety have been quick to recognize the threats posed by their "unofficial" rivals, and in this recognition they have acknowledged in fact—whether or not they have withheld the honorific label of "religion" from their rival—the religious potency of many apparently secular phenomena. This potency—the fundamental potency of any functioning religion—is at the level of primary values. Religion is first of all a matter of "worthship." Religion is basically a way of valuing—or, better, of being grasped by a sense of worth that transcends all other seeming worths and comprehends every true worth. Religion is our most intensive and comprehensive way of valuing.[6]

But valuing is itself fundamental to every aspect of our life. What we find intensely worthy, as in the act of worship, pervades our *feelings,* of course. But valuing is not limited to the domain of feeling alone. *Perception* itself has been shown to be intimately tied to primary, often preconscious valuation. I shall return to develop this point in later chapters; for now it should suffice merely to recall that perception is always selective, based on an implicit judgment of importance. The organism lives—sees and hears as well as feels—by its basic values. *Belief,* too, at the dynamic interface of perception, emotion, and action, is also profoundly relevant to our life as valuers; and, obviously, what we *do,* how we behave, is public expression of our functioning value structures.

Therefore, if religion is at heart a value phenomenon, it carries with it inevitably the whole self in all its aspects— feeling, perceiving, thinking, and acting. And indeed we find that all religions reach into, and organize, life at all these levels. There are characteristic attitudes and *feelings* associated with every religion; each religion guides its adherents to *see* the world in its characteristic way; thought, *beliefs* (often, though not always, logically systematized "doctrine") play a part in all religions; and characteristic *behavior,* ritually and/or ethically supported, is universally present as well.

One virtue of approaching religion from a broad functional perspective and identifying its root as "worthship" is the freedom it gives from the common intellectualistic error of identifying religion with doctrine. Some intellectual content is always present, as we have seen, since persons are conscious, thinking beings. But religion is not first of all a way of thinking, much less of formal theologizing; religion is first of all a way of responding to intimations of worth—responding totally, humanly, not excluding ideas therefore, but not first of all responding by systematic doctrine. Systematic doctrine comes later, if it comes at all. And systematic doctrine—logical theology—when it is associated with a religious tradition as, for example, in Christianity, is in the service of those more basic intimations of worth which constitute the religious consciousness. In chapter 5, I shall deal more fully with the importance of these theological functions. But here the central point to recognize is that on the ideational side of religion the *basic* intimations are to be found expressed not in theology but in the value-drenched stories and images associated with relatively unformalized thought. Such images, vivid pictures, stories, tales, etc., together constitute a shifting, potent mosaic worldview (not necessarily logically consistent but mythopoetically coherent) which expresses and reinforces the values of the devoted community. This is the mythic matrix from which the full religious phenomenon—combining feeling, perception, belief and action—arises, and to which all aspects of the religious phenomenon return for reinforcement and renewal.

By *myth,* of course, I intend no suggestion of falsity. Popular usage of this sort is shallow. Rather I define *myth* (or *mythos*) in terms of its depth functions: of representing paradigms for fundamental values and of proffering answers to fundamental uncertainties. Treating *mythos* in this fashion opens the way to appreciative study and discriminating criticism that is prevented by literalist assumptions. An important way into the understanding of any basic religious phenomena will consequently be through the mythic matrix, if we can find it.

The practical importance of identifying the mythic matrix is considerable if our interest is in observing how societies form their fundamental characters and shape their basic policies of action. R. M. MacIver put it well:

> By *myths* we mean the value-impregnated beliefs and notions that men hold, that they live by or live for. Every society is held together by a myth-system, a complex of dominating thought-forms that determines and sustains all its activities. All social relations, the very texture of human society, are myth-born and myth sustained. . . . When we speak here of myth we imply nothing concerning the grounds of belief, so far as belief claims to interpret reality. We use the word in an entirely neutral sense.[7]

From central values, from the functioning religion of a culture, behavior naturally follows, as we have seen; and collective behavior patterns, coupled with common fundamental goals and common fundamental ways of perceiving the world, constitute for better or for worse civilizations like the classical Greek or the medieval, the Hindu or the modern world, whose spiritual roots we shall soon be attempting to trace and whose spiritual successor we shall then be attempting to envision.

What is the mythic matrix of the modern world? What are the images that for roughly three centuries have expressed and reinforced the characteristic values of modern consciousness? If we can begin to find our way into these questions, we will be in a position to explore their implications more fully in the following chapters.

Earlier I noted that the origins of the modern world in the seventeenth century were simultaneous with the origins of modern science. This was no mere coincidence. Typical scientific practices and early methodological decisions suggested (and were generated by) images of how things basically are and ought to be. These images together constituted the potent mythic matrix that gave rise, when systematized, to the metaphysic of scientism. The scientistic worldview, eventually accepted in gross form as the common sense of modernity, has structured the consciousness of the modern world. Since human consciousness is always deeply laden with value intimations, the spiritual virtues and vices implicit in scientific practice have become the spiritual virtues and vices of the modern world.

In this way modern science, besides being a secular set of particular practices designed to provide specific answers to limited questions, became the generator of a religious movement that vanquished one civilization, the medieval, and gave birth to a new world in its own image. The crisis of the passing away in our time of this modern world so generated is, therefore, the crisis of modern science extended beyond inquiry to theophany, the crisis of scientism as mythic matrix for our lives. The nub of the search for a livable post-modern world is the task of finding a worthy successor for scientistic consciousness without abandoning the genuine virtues of science itself.

Thus stands my thesis, simply stated. Telling the story more fully gets more complicated.

First, it should not be supposed that the worldview of modern science owed nothing to the *mythos* of Christian consciousness in which the former gestated through centuries of noteworthy premodern scientific practice. I cannot here discuss the long preparation, though it is a most impressive story being told with ever-increasing respect by contemporary historians of science. Even without the details, however, modern science could hardly be imagined—and in historical fact, of course, never did arise—apart from an incubation in a prior *mythos* which the Christian picture of the world supplied. That Christian—more accurately I should say biblical—picture shows God, the rational creator, omnipotently ruling the universe in every minute detail.

Think of the possible alternatives. One might picture a visible universe full of mere happenings with no significant order or merely illusory oder. Such a picture of the natural order is what is reflected in Hindu consciousness of *maya,* the tricky (*magic* comes from the same root)—the half-real unstable surface of appearances. Such consciousness could support no investment of effort in scientific observation or meticulous search for underlying laws. Such a way of perceiving the world would never lead one to notice nature as predictable, manipulable—or, indeed, worth predicting and manipulating.

Another picture of the universe might depict God as creator and omnipotent ruler over nature, but omit from the picture (and thus from the matrix of supreme values) the rationality of God—his steadiness, faithfulness, regularity. Such an image might represent God's rule over nature as arbitrary or, from the human viewpoint, capricious. And, indeed, the Islamic consciousness of Allah is of such a character. God's sovereignty must permit radical unpredictability; God's inscrutable will is near the center of Islamic veneration. In such a matrix of religious imagery, despite its proven capacity to generate high culture and splendid scholarship, the prerequisites for scientific practice were not present.

To take a third example, we can easily imagine a *mythos* in which the ultimate powers, though rational, are not in full control over nature. Perhaps they are in conflict with another contrary power, as in the Zoroastrian vision of the universe;

perhaps, as in forms of Gnosticism and neo-Platonism, there are inherent limits in what can be done with the recalcitrant and imperfect material world. In any of these cases the basis for scientific work, which as Alfred North Whitehead puts it, "instinctively holds that all things great and small are conceivable as exemplifications of general principles which reign throughout the natural order,"[8] simply is absent.

The Christian *mythos,* however, uniquely provided the combination of values which could support the birth of modern science. Christian Europe alone developed what Whitehead describes as "the inexpugnable belief that every detailed occurrence can be correlated with its antecedents in a perfectly definite manner, exemplifying general principles."[9] And this value-laden belief has profound consequences for practice. "Without this belief," Whitehead goes on, "the incredible labours of scientists would be without hope. It is this instinctive conviction, vividly poised before the imagination, which is the motive power of research—that there is a secret, a secret which can be unveiled."[10] The possibility of this conviction, however, rests on the kind of God who emerges from the telling of biblical stories combined with the valuing of Greek rationality that entered Christian consciousness at a very early point. Whitehead again expresses the argument succinctly.

> When we compare this tone of thought in Europe with the attitude of other civilizations when left to themselves, there seems but one source for its origin. It must come from the medieval insistence on the rationality of God, conceived as with the personal energy of Jehovah and with the rationality of a Greek philosopher. Every detail was supervised and ordered: the search into nature could only result in the vindication of the faith in rationality. Remember that I am not talking of the explicit beliefs of a few individuals. What I mean is the impress on the European mind arising from the unquestioned faith of centuries. By this I mean the instinctive tone of thought and not a mere creed of words.[11]

The "impress" that Whitehead speaks of was essential for the birth of modern scientific practice; but, as we know, the "impress" of the new, once born, led to images of reality inconsistent with the old Christian picture and then led to its gradual replacement as the "instinctive tone of thought"— what I have been calling the mythic matrix—in Europe and then, largely, in the rest of the world.

The story of the triumph of modern consciousness is old and often told. It involves calling off the roster of the spiritual heroes of our culture: Galileo, Newton, Darwin, Freud, Einstein —and the multitude of the faithful servants of objective truth, unnamed hosts of witnesses to the spiritual power of the modern vision finally ascendant.

In the beginning the struggle between alternative visions of reality, with their profound value implications, was clear and dramatic. Galileo, the Copernican visionary, confronted the established representatives of Christian *mythos* with a dramatic intensity that continues to ring down the ages. On reading Galileo it becomes evident that two "world systems" (as he called them) are indeed in rivalry. Two grand images of reality, not just two theories of astronomy or different views about dynamics, are locked in deadly combat. The diplomatic maneuvering, the legal niceties, the attempts at compromise that surrounded that controversy seem strangely irrelevant once this is seen. There can be no compromise when the center of the sacred—the mythic matrix—is at stake. For Galileo, a whole new set of values was represented by the picture of the universe he saw and advocated—the Earth no longer seen as sundered absolutely and qualitatively from the heavens, but now itself as much a "heavenly body" (note the value implications!) as Jupiter or the Moon; the laws of motion written in the precise and universal language of mathematics instead of the vague anthropocentric abstractions of the Aristotelian schoolmen; and the authority of unfettered reasoning and empirical observation affirmed over the massive weight of tradition or institutional coercion.

Tradition and coercion seemed to win that time, of course. But the victory was costly and transient. Galileo's vision could not be confined by house arrest, and the saga of scientific imagery gradually shaping modern consciousness is well known to all. Again and again biblical pictures of the world were forced from the field in unseemly disarray after initial struggle. Newton vanquished lingering opposition in astronomy or physics with the towering genius of his mechanical world-picture. Darwin confounded believers in the special creation of humanity with his overwhelmingly compelling vision of vastly expanded time frames and the purposeless mechanism of natural selection. Freud tore away the sanctuary of the human psyche, replacing the image of God in ourselves with a disturbingly different image. Einstein turned our universe into a strange, unfamiliar place of warping space-time fields and of matter made from energy.

By the mid-twentieth century the triumph of the scientistic worldview was at a climax. Voices of dissent were occasionally heard, of course, but modernity had never been so nearly unanimous. The magic wand of scientific technology had transformed the world, provided more bread than ever before in history; established round-the-clock circuses on television; healed the sick; restored hearing to the deaf; reached the Moon; explained the thunder; and was giving promise of life abundant for all—eliminating the curse of Adam —on and on into the indefinitely progressive future.

Little wonder, then, that the authority of modern scientistic consciousness was overwhelming, even among the uneducated who have never been known for sophisticated scientific thinking but who accept their functioning religious imagery from whatever priests seem best in touch with the Powers That Be. The authority of the laboratory coat—even when worn by an actor and seen merely in image on a television tube—has been well exploited by those who seek profit from the faithfulness of the multitudes.

Not merely the multitudes, however, but the intelligentsia were mainly won by the scientistic worldview in the mid-twentieth century. In philosophy the dominant Anglo-American movement was either logical positivism, which made itself explicitly into the handmaiden of scientific practice, or forms of analysis spun off from logical positivism and retaining characteristic preference for clarity, precision, and for dividing problems into their minimum parts. And in Christian theology itself, to make this victory of modern consciousness complete, the progressive young theologians of midcentury were rejoicing in the secular city (Cox), and were announcing religionless Christianity (Bonhoeffer), Christ without myth (Ogden), the secular meaning of the gospel (van Buren), and, of course, the death of God (Hamilton, Altizer).

The triumph was nearly complete. The tide of modern consciousness had engulfed us all. Many of us are still modern, for that matter, in what Whitehead call the "instinctive tone of our thought" and feel the high values in genuine science with deep poignancy. There is so much that is noble in the strivings after clarity and objective truth, precision, and warranted fact. Must the scientific enterprise itself be tarred with the excesses of modern civilization?

Notes

1. Kenneth E. Boulding, *The Meaning of the Twentieth Century: The Great Transition* (New York: Harper & Row, 1964), p. 100.

2. Dennis Meadows et al., *The Limits to Growth* (New York: Universe Books, 1972), p. 29.

3. *See* Garrett Hardin, "The Case Against Helping the Poor," *Psychology Today,* September 1974, p. 38 ff.

4. *See,* for example, *Models of Doom: A Critique of The Limits to Growth,* ed. H. S. D. Cole et al. (New York: Universe Books, 1973).

5. For greater detail and defense *see* my *Basic Modern Philosophy of Religion* (New York: Charles Scribner, 1967), parts 1 and 3.

6. Ibid., chap. 3.

7. R. M. MacIver, *The Web of Government* (New York: Macmillan, 1947), p. 4.

8. Alfred North Whitehead, *Science and the Modern World* (New York: The Free Press, 1967), p. 5.

9. Ibid., p. 12.

10. Ibid.

11. Ibid.

2. ALIEN UNIVERSE

Let me confess: I have always liked and admired science.
When in grade school I was named class "science reporter"
because I had taken up reading science books in the local
library after school (while evading the neighborhood bully). It
is an amateur interest that has never left me, even without
being bullied into it. Technology, too, has always pleased and
fascinated me. I used to love to tinker with wires and batteries;
now, as a pilot and aircraft maintainer I find I have deep
aesthetic as well as practical admiration for airplanes and the
gadgets that go into them. In college I was a "science fiction
freak"; I still can hardly believe summer has begun until I have
opened my vacation with a good science fiction yarn.

I make these personal remarks because I do not want my
thesis to be overinterpreted. My position, briefly, is as follows:
that science was the most potent agency that formed the
consciousness of the modern world; that there are fatal flaws
in the modern world which make its ending certain; that these
flaws are directly traceable to flaws in modern consciousness;

and, therefore, that science when functioning beyond its secular limits as mythic matrix of our obsolescent culture is itself signifiantly flawed.

I

First, is it clear that scientific practice is capable of being extended to generate a spiritual vision? I shall argue that this is indeed the case, and that the scientistic vision is at the root of much that is characteristic of modern culture.

Any fundamental religious phenomenon, as I held in the previous chapter, is organized by deeply felt values issuing in characteristic behavior that is considered linked to the "sacred" or ultimately worthy. Sometimes it is difficult or impossible to distinguish whether the linkage is a ritual or an ethical one. Abstaining from meat on Fridays, when this was required of Roman Catholics, seems a pretty clear case of a ritual linkage, while abstaining from adultery, for example, seems a pretty obvious case of ethical linkage. But the categories have a way of merging under some circumstances. Many strict Catholics felt moral compunctions about meatless Fridays—and is it not an ethical failing to violate one's duty of obedience to legitimate ecclesiastical discipline? One old monk, I am told, felt so deeply about the prohibition that the first Friday it was lifted (by legitimate ecclesiastical authority) he refused to eat the celebration steaks served by the monastery cooks: "The Holy Father can go to hell if he wishes," he moaned, "but I'll not eat meat on Friday." Such "scrupulosity," as Catholic moral theologians call it, even where no ethical point seems at issue, is a good sign that we have entered a religious context, where valuing is intense and zealotry is always only a step away from zeal.

Likewise indicative of religious dynamics at work are those cases where what looks like ethical injunctions function like ritual ones. Refraining from adultery, normally, is an ethical policy with much ethical point. But under some circumstances, where the ethical point is lost, the prohibition, if regarded, serves instead as a ritual. To take an extreme example from a science fiction story I read long ago, the plot entailed that the entire population of the world had somehow been wiped out except for two adult human beings, a man and a woman. The human race would perish unless they had children who could begin to replenish the world. But, alas, the couple were not married and there were no clergymen left alive to tie the sanctifying knot. The man was willing to risk it, but the woman took the Seventh Commandment absolutely. The world ended, as I recall, with a whimper.

It is not easy to draw a line, then, when sacred values are at stake, between behavior relevant to such values linked by ethical or by ritual sanctions. Let us, however, as a very rough rule of thumb say that ritual action is action relevant to sacred values which is performed for its own sake or as a symbol of the ultimately worthy. Let us say that religiously sanctioned ethical action is action relevant to sacred values which is performed for the furtherance of some religiously valued end or good. Then I believe we can see that scientific practice involves both sacred ritual and religiously sanctioned ethics.

A *ritual* of science would involve a way of doing things whose propriety is deeply felt to touch on the ultimately worthy which is valued for its own sake, regardless of whether good is gained or lost thereby. One such sacred ritual, present since Descartes' famous founding of modern thought in methodological doubt, is deliberate suspense of judgment in the absence of sufficient evidence. Scientific thinkers must not believe anything to any degree more strongly than the objective evidence warrants, even if it means failing to believe something that is in fact true, and missing, to that extent, the good end of maximizing the stock of true beliefs. The bad-in-itself, avoided by this sacred ritual, is credulity, the state of consciousness most disvalued by the scientific community. The good-in-itself, symbolized by and implicit in this central ritual, is critical objectivity.

The most famous defense of such ritual scrupulosity, despite the possible loss of truth, was made by W. K. Clifford in the nineteenth century when he wrote: "If I let myself believe anything on insufficient evidence, there may be no great harm done by the mere belief; it may be true after all, or I may never have occasion to exhibit it in outward acts. But I cannot help doing this great wrong towards Man, that I make myself credulous."[1]

Most of us now, I am sure, share Clifford's disapproval of credulity. We admire critical objectivity as an intrinsically valuable state of consciousness. We are, after all, dwellers in the latter days of the modern world sharing most of the values that science-generated objective consciousness has victoriously instilled throughout our culture. But we should at least notice that Clifford's argument, though we may instinctively nod when we hear it, supports a mode of behavior that other types of consciousness might not find self-evidently valuable at all. Belief without objective evidence—belief, that is, by subjective hunch, by poetic suggestion, by authority of shaman, by sheer delight in what is believed, by fear of disbelief, by social solidarity, by moral duty, by love or loyalty or the like—such believing is an ever-present human possibility which under different value priorities might be affirmed as far better than critically objective suspense of judgment. What, it might be asked, is so absolute about objective consciousness *as such* that it merits losing the potential values of believing beyond or without evidence? What is so sacred about ritual avoidance of credulity that it makes modern scientistic consciousness prefer to lose friendship, or beauty, or even truth itself, perhaps, rather than to profane objectivity?

These, if uttered, would be basic rival religious challenges to basic science-generated religious values. We should not expect a ready answer, since the highest value can never—in principle—be justified. As highest, it is the ground of all justification. To attempt to justify it by some other value would be to make the other value higher; it can only be justified by itself, therefore, which means that it is beyond the context of justification. Thus we must view scientific ritual avoidance of credulity as touching upon a functioning religious ultimate, symbolizing and incarnating the intensely valued objective-critical consciousness itself.

I have started at the top, as it were, of the ritual hierarchy in scientific practice. But even minor practices reflect the centrality of sanctified objective consciousness. There is, for example, a ritual way of writing up experimental reports that strikes me as portentous, for all its familiarity. The ritual is to write everything in the passive voice, with all references to the experimenter eliminated, if possible, but if not, at least transformed into the third person. All first person remarks or actions are systematically eliminated. Instead of: "Then I put the test tube into the Bunsen burner while glancing at the clock," we are taught to write: "Next, the test tube was introduced into the flame and the time noted." Men and women don't see or hear or smell things; on this ritual "observations are made." People don't put things on scales or place rulers against things: "measurements are performed." The ritual of scientific writing style systematically impersonalizes. Why? Is there any practical or ethical point to such a formal practice? I suspect that neither clarity nor precision would need to be sacrificed in a laboratory report that used first-person active language;[2] but the mood, the tone, the subliminal feel would be very different. And so would the symbolism, which now works to cultivate a consciousness in which the peculiarities of individual subjectivities count not at all. The persons who do or see or measure don't matter; what matters, as symbolized and reinforced by the ritual language, are the objective events, the recorded observations, the performed measurements. It is negligible that some particular person did this or that; it is important only that this or that happened under carefully defined circumstances. The ritual writing style of science, though a minor symbol, no doubt, points to the sacred value matrix of objective consciousness and participates in it as well.

Ritual, as I said earlier, is not clearly distinguishable from ethics when both rise from the same ultimate value center, but I have attempted to give instances that seem to me mainly drawn from the ritual side of science as a functioning religious phenomenon. Now let me comment on science-generated consciousness as profoundly under moral authority as well. Some persistently confuse the ideal of *objectivity* in scientific practice with moral *neutrality*. Nothing could be farther apart. The ideal of objectivity of science is the ground of powerful moral commitments. As Israel Scheffler writes in *Science and Subjectivity* (a passionate polemic in defense of objective consciousness): "A major aspect of [its] significance has been the moral import of science: its dynamic articulation of the impulse to responsible belief, and its suggestion of the hope of an increased rationality and responsibility in all realms of conduct and thought."[3]

This moral import, Scheffler argues, is particularly expressed in the demand of objective consciousness for belief based on controls independent of any person's wishes. He opens his book with the sentence: "A fundamental feature of science is its ideal of objectivity, an ideal that subjects all scientific statements to the test of independent and impartial criteria, recognizing no authority of persons in the realm of cognition."[4] Like St. Paul's depiction of God, objective consciousness is "no respecter of persons" (Rom. 2:11). Our duties are to obey no final authority but critical reason. This valuation is not merely intensive but also comprehensive. Objective consciousness is not only to be the highest authority in explicitly scientific contexts but in all domains. This Scheffler refers to as "the underlying moral impulse of positivism,"[5] and goes on to spell out the positivist unity of science doctrine as follows: "to affirm the responsibilities of assertion no matter what the subject matter, to grant no holidays from such responsibilities for the humanities, politics, or the social sciences in particular, despite their strong capacities for arousing emotion and stimulating partisanship."[6]

Thus a comprehensive morality of impartiality, self-control, personal accountability, and democratic antiauthoritarianism rises out of objective consciousness, and we recognize it, I think, as worthy of our respect. These are high values, are they not? They are values we wish we could attain for ourselves and our society.

Jacob Bronowski develops his list of the values springing from the quest for objective truth yet further. In *Science and Human Values* he identifies moral traits that are essential for the very existence of science. The objective quest requires respect for *independence,* he notes, because where there is responsible belief each must think his own thoughts and judge evidence for himself. There must further be a high place for *originality,* if novel truths are to emerge. Independence and originality will result in dissent, of course, which means that a morality rising from objective consciousness will need to value *freedom of expression, tolerance,* and mutual *respect.* All the virtues of modern liberal democracy, in fact, are implicit in the practice of science; the vices we still see around us, Bronowski urges, are cultural holdovers from premodern credulous ages and institutions.[7]

II

I hope by now that I have succeeded in my first aim of this chapter: namely, in replacing what Scheffler calls the "myth" of the "cold, aloof scientist"[8] with some sense—however sketchy—of the vibrant valuational power implicit in scientific enterprises. What seems cold to others is passionate self-discipline in the service of sacred and rigorous clarity; what seems aloof is dedication to impersonal standards by which objectivity is maintained. Objective truth is the end; objective reason is the means. End and means cohere and reinforce one another, vision and practice, ritual and morality —into a unity that makes objective consciousness the motivating center of a major functioning religious phenomenon.

By asserting that it is a functioning religious phenomenon, of course, I do not mean to suggest that the modern world actually lives fully by or through the ideals of objectivity. No more did medieval people live fully by or through the ideals of Christianity. But as Christianity—fully exemplified only in a few saints, supported by priests and ecclesiastical institutions, and generally accepted at the instinctive level as authorative by the bulk of medieval society—put what Whitehead call its "impress" on the thought, feelings, perceptions, and characteristic institutions of Christendom, so objective consciousness—fully exemplified only in a few scientific heroes, supported by working researchers and their institutions, and generally accepted at the instinctive level as authoritative by the bulk of modern people—has put its "impress" on the thought, feelings, perceptions and characteristic institutions of modernity whenever and wherever in its progressive expansion the modern world has reached.

It is appropriate, then, to trace the impact of scientism on our cultural history—that is, how this phenomenon has manifested its most basic traits in the institutions, the policies, and the character of the modern world—just as historians trace the impact of Christianity on medieval Christendom. In this project I shall select three basic traits of scientific practice for attention: connecting each to the value-laden images of reality that extend scientific practice into a mythic vision; illustrating each from the work of Galileo, as "saint" and "martyr"; and tracing each to consequences in the modern world around us that show the valuational limits of scientism's objective consciousness—and that spell practical ruin as well.

First, an essential trait of objective consciousness, as we have seen, is its requirement that *belief be strictly tied to objective evidence.* No merely private whim, hunch or feeling is to be allowed standing in the court of objective reason. Without such a requirement it is impossible to conceive of modern science as we have known it.

Galileo grasped this point unerringly. What counts as objective evidence is what can be tested by public methods of weighing, timing, measuring. These characteristics of things can be quantified, checked, and rechecked by anyone, regardless of mood or other private, subjective considerations. More generally, any merely subjective aspects of experience must be irrelevant to the steady progress toward objective truth. What is merely personal or private is unconfirmable, unmeasurable, and secondary for scientific purposes. What will be primary for purposes of providing objective evidence will be aspects of reality that can be checked on by others (that is, "public" aspects of things) and that allow precise, quantitative measurement.

Galileo consequently introduced (and Descartes greatly elaborated) a vital distinction required by objective consciousness between the *primary* qualities of things and their *secondary* qualities. The primary qualities of, say, a billiard ball will be its weight, or massiveness, its shape or figure, its motion (including both quantity of time and quantity of distance covered); the secondary qualities will consist, among others, in the shade of color we perceive, or the quality of the sound we hear when one ball strikes another, or the texture as we feel it on our palm. These latter are all qualitative, not quantitative. They are not public and confirmable. What quality of color you see is private to your subjective awareness. Perhaps you are color-blind. Perhaps the quality you privately experience and call "green" is in fact the quality I privately experience and call "red." How could we ever know? What difference would it make?

Moreover, all such qualities seem to be produced by my subjective interaction with the objective world. If a tree falls in the forest and no one is there to hear, so the most famous philosophical puzzle of the modern world runs, is there any sound? The obvious answer, given Galileo's distinction, is that in the sense of "sound" in which *primary* features are understood—the interactions of material bodies with shape and weight, the setting into measurable motion of particles dancing as sound waves pass—there *is* sound; but in the sense of "sound" in which the *quality* of the crackling branches is meant, there obviously is only silence. For the totally deaf (and for the world itself) there are no sounds, only vibrations. The vibrations, as primary qualities, are consequently the objectively real features of the universe; qualities of tone are merely subjective.

The real world, the objectively true world, consequently, is made up of what can be apart from the private irrelevancies of human subjectivity. Just as there is no *pain* in the objective fire, but only in my awareness if I let my body get too close, so by the same token there is no *warmth,* in the sense that I feel its comforting glow. What there really is, in what we subjectively call heat, is more or less rapid movement (measurable) of tiny molecules (with mass and length and shape). Color, as we of the modern world all believe, is "really" only electromagnetic vibrations, and different hues are "really" only different frequencies on a spectrum of energetic wave phenomena that extends well above and well below the narrow range called visible light, where human subjectivity alone supplies the many-hued rainbow.

This is a compelling image, and one that rises directly and essentially from objective methods. It is familiar. It enters into our authoritative vision of the universe. What is real and basic is the measurable, the material. What is suspect and relative is the qualitative, the private, the merely mental. Thus, at last, if the sound of the tree in the forest and the colors of the rainbow must be credited to the human mind, not to the objective world, so much more must the values we experience along with them—the thrilling dissonance of the crash or the subtle beauty of the rainbow. If the tree-in-the-forest problem is the modern world's most famous and characteristic metaphysical saw, the most characteristic aesthetic cliché comes out of the same consciousness: "Beauty is in the eye of the beholder." And so, of course, must all values be in a world devoid of quality. Whitehead sadly sums it up: "Nature is a dull affair, soundless, scentless, colourless; merely the hurrying of material, endlessly, meaninglessly."[9]

Protests against this vision of the world, including Whitehead's protest, have been heard. Various lines of criticism have been taken. Whitehead, for instance, argues that it is simply unbelievable. He marshals evidence from poetic insight to show that the basic, concrete data of human experience are overwhelmingly in opposition. Then he concludes that between concrete data of experience and mere theory, one must side with the data and conclude that the theory is wrong. I agree with Whitehead in principle: theoretical abstraction must give way to concrete experience. But I wonder whether Whitehead takes seriously enough the fact I have been stressing here: that for the modern consciousness this is no mere theory to be used or discarded at will, but, instead, this has become a value-laden vision of reality—a way of feeling and relating to the universe. We shall require not merely a different theory—though new theory will be needed—but a change of consciousness itself in order to experience the world another way.

Another critic recently has been Lewis Mumford, whose attack has been from the standpoint of morality. The "crime of Galileo" was to alienate humanity from the fullness of our own experience as well as from our universe. It was not so much merely to break with the authority of the Church but, worse, to break down respect for personality. As Mumford writes:

> By his exclusive preoccupation with quantity Galileo had, in affect, *disqualified* the real world of experience; and he had thus driven man out of living nature into a cosmic desert, even more peremptorily than Jehovah had driven Adam and Eve out of the Garden of Eden. But in Galileo's case the punishment for eating the apple of the tree of knowledge lay in the nature of knowledge itself, for that tasteless, dessicated fruit was incapable of sustaining or reproducing life. . . .
>
> From the seventeenth century on, the technological world,

which prided itself on reducing or extruding the human personality, progressively replaced both nature and human culture and claimed indeed a higher status for itself, as the concrete working-model of scientific truth. "In 1893," Loren Eiseley reminds us, "Robert Monro in an opening address before the British Association for the Advancement of Science remarked sententiously . . . 'imagination, conceptions, idealizations, the moral faculties . . . may be compared to parasites that live at the expense of their neighbors.' " To have pointed the way to this devaluation of the personality, and its eventual exile, was the real crime of Galileo.[10]

To Whitehead's epistemological warning and Mumford's passionate moral protest, I would like to add a word on the practical social consequences of this aspect of scientistic *mythos*. It has, through its world picture with its implicit values, reinforced the supreme importance of the "hardheaded" in modern institutions and policies. What really counts is the countable—the measurable, the tangible, the material. The objective consciousness of the modern world can count money, size, output, speed. "More," "bigger," "faster" become transcendent and unexaminable values drawn from fundamental functioning religious imagery and supportive of tendencies toward greed, conflict, and war. Likewise, as I shall discuss more fully in the next chapter, modern consciousness puts its faith in its hardware—to preserve it from military destruction and ecological collapse. To challenge this instinctive faith in the "technological fix" is to challenge something very deep in our souls. Most of us cannot even imagine another way. In the same way we find it hard to take values other than measurable material values with any great degree of seriousness. The pervasive *ugliness* of the modern world wherever it has spread—from Jersey City to Japan—is one of its most obvious features. It is slightly unfair to compare a medieval cathedral with a modern oil refinery, but not entirely so. These are typical institutions of their respective civilizations and they well represent where the basic values have been invested. Aesthetic considerations in our modern world are arbitrarily split off from the rest of life and are supposed to be left for the women (and effete poets, environmentalists or other such weaklings), while the real world pursues real interests: that is, economic ones. Wherever material, quantifiable, "real" values (jobs, production, income) are threatened by merely subjective, qualitative concerns, the people tend to recoil and their politicians with them.

Conflict, obsessive material consumption, adulation of growth, and pervasive ugliness are not the only social consequences of the modern *mythos*. In addition, the objective world without intrinsic values becomes mere resource pit and dumping ground. There are no values in the objective world to slow us down. Pollution is in the eye of the beholder. And so it is, painfully! And so it will be, increasingly, until it becomes—as we must hope it is not already—too late to turn back from ecological collapse. One consequence of objective consciousness, then is *alienation from quality in the universe* with all that this portends for human life.

The supreme value of objectivity requires public evidence, as we have seen, but second, it demands *rigorous clarity* as well. The muddling of things together that can be seen dispassionately apart is the enemy of scientific reason. Scientific practice leads to *analysis* of its subject matter, therefore, and best of all to mathematical analysis with its power and precision.

Galileo, again, led the way:

Philosophy is written in this grand book, the universe, which stands continually open to our gaze. But the book cannot be understood unless one first learns to comprehend the language and read the letters in which it is composed. It is written in the language of mathematics, and its characters are triangles, circles, and other geometric figures, without which it is humanly impossible to understand a single word of it; without them, one wanders about in a dark labyrinth.[11]

To understand the whole, divide the problem, Descartes urged modern thinkers, and analyze it in terms of the mathematics of its smallest components. The objective truth will become clear when these elements are distinctly known, together with the quantifiable laws of their combination.

The stress of early modern scientific practice on clarity through analysis gives us more than a method to follow, it also gives us a vivid image of how things are, fundamentally: things are aggregates of tiny parts which have laws of their own, by virtue of which the larger wholes are constructed. The more basic reality is the tiny part, obviously, and the derivative reality is the compound everyday object, the resultant of many parts working according to their laws.

The cell is more basic than the whole living body, on this worldview; the molecule is more basic than the living cell; the atoms of the molecule are more basic than the molecule; and the subatomic particles—electrons, protons, and all the other swarm—are more basic than the atom. They are the "ultimately real." But of course they are not living. Thus nonlife is more ultimate than life, and physics is the fundamental science in every sense: it deals with the fundamental particles of which everything is derived, and it is in principle fundamental to all the sciences which, one by one, reduce to physics. Sociology, that is, reduces to individual psychology; psychology reduces to brain physiology and general biology; biology reduces to molecular chemistry; and chemistry in its turn reduces to the subject matter of physics.

This familiar imagery of reductionism coheres well with the objective world-picture of quantifiable material in motion and refines it still further. The most important of the material realities are the smallest particles. All else is derivative and secondary. And therefore the kinds of properties that fundamental particles have are basic to the universe. That rules out life as having any basic status, of course, and further locks mind, the ephemeral third-order by-product of the physical universe, firmly into its subjective limbo. Perhaps subjectivity isn't even there at all, muse some extreme reductionists.

Reductive analysis, however, though implicit in objective consciousness, contains seeds of its own destruction. I do not refer, merely, to the obvious awkwardness of a living being devoting intense efforts of thought in attempting to show that he or she is neither living nor thinking. That would be a tactic successful only against those few who hold that derivative realities are not real at all, but are mere illusions. Most reductive analysts do not take this extreme position, though admittedly they then have the difficult task of explaining where phenomena like life and subjectivity—apparently ungrounded in the basic realities of the universe—can possibly come from. I will not press the fact, either, that reduction is not an accomplished scientific achievement but only a program believed to be possible in the assumed progressive future of objective consciousness. There have been remarkable reductionist successes. The science of thermodynamics has been reduced to that of statistical mechanics; and molecular biology is currently showing new relationships between genetic stability and molecular chemistry. Such relationships should, after all, be expected in a unified world.

What is fatal about reductionist analysis is its claim to be exhaustive and complete in its vision. But this is impossible in principle, as Michael Polanyi stresses.[12] Before we begin to analyze an interesting whole, he points out, we must first be able to recognize the whole as interesting. Any consciousness operating by analysis alone could never recognize the difference between the atoms of the frog and of the fly and of the air and water surrounding them. We must—logically must —move *from* holistic awareness of significant unities, *then* to the detailed parts that find their meaning and importance in the wholes within which they function, if we are to understand the universe as it is. Unless we get the *Gestalt* of things first, the process of analysis would never give us unities again.

To this logical point I would like to add another practical dimension which arises when analysis claims exclusive adequacy for consciousness. The ecosphere within which we dwell is a delicately woven web of life. To be understood— more urgently, to be saved from collapse—this vulnerable and immensely complex network must be approached holistically, contrary to the habits of modern analytical consciousness. The consequences of our failures to think and perceive our world in multivalent rather than analytically monovalent ways are already painfully apparent. Barry Commoner repeatedly points these out in *The Closing Circle* and names the proper culprit. Regarding the complex holistic chemistry of air pollution, for example, he writes:

> In order to describe the course of a particular chemical reaction, it is necessary to study it in isolation, separate from other processes that might change the reaction under study. However if, for the sake of such an analysis, a few ingredients are isolated from the mixture of polluted air, this artificial change destroys precisely the complex of chemical reaction that needs to be understood. This is the ultimate theoretical limitation.[13]

An ultimate theoretical limitation? Yes, at least as long as scientistic consciousness remains intent on analysis as the only possible sort of responsible thought. Genuine science may be leaving the typically modern scientistic *mythos* behind, of course, since exclusive emphasis on analysis and reduction is being replaced by holistic systems approaches in certain frontier sciences, notably in ecology itself. I shall have more to say about the possibility of post-modern forms of science later in this book; but here it is important to recognize the continuing pervasiveness of reductive analysis and professional overspecialization as dangerous legacies from the modern *mythos.* The danger, as Commoner shows, is in continuing to relate to our environment through technologies (and policies) that themselves arise from reductive-analytical modes of consciousness.

In sum, we can trace the origin of the environmental crisis through the following sequence. Environmental degradation largely results from the introduction of new industrial and agricultural technologies. These technologies are ecologically faulty because they are designed to solve singular, separate problems and fail to take account of the inevitable "side effects" that arise because, in nature, no part is isolated from the whole ecological fabric. In turn, the fragmented design of technology reflects its scientific foundation, for science is divided into disciplines that are largely governed by the notion that complex systems can be understood only if they are first broken into their separate component parts. This reductionist bias has also tended to shield basic science from a concern for real-life problems, such as environmental degradation.[14]

The modern world, then, has alienated itself dangerously from the natural environment on which all, ultimately, depend for life. This has been done enthusiastically through the very successes of modern technology, the practical offspring of modern science. We are alienated not merely because we deny intrinsic value to the real world, not merely because we are obsessed with material growth and heedless of the ugliness we spread. We are alienated—and in imminent danger of terrible retribution for our self-alienation—because we have not thought or felt or perceived holistically but rather have torn into the delicate web of life with tubular vision, reductionist assumptions, and exclusively analytical logic. Our tools of objective consciousness have been powerful, but their very effectiveness, ironically, is leading remorselessly to the undoing of the modern world.

Finally, before turning in the next chapter to technology itself as a religious phenomenon, I shall note a third scientific practice extended dangerously into religious vision. Objectivity is no respecter of persons, as we have seen. On one level this stands for fearless independence in the facts of intimidating authority; on another level, we discover, this stands for deep-seated disregard for personality and its subjective traits. In the latter sense the methodological decisions of modern science may be seen as fueling a consistent attack *against anthropocentric and anthropomorphic visions of the universe.*

Galileo battled anthropocentrism when he argued for the Copernican displacement of the earth from the center of the astronomical picture; he also battled anthropomorphism when he fought Aristotelian dynamics with its baggage of "final causes." The stone does not fall to the earth because it is "seeking" its own proper place, Galileo argued; and it does not accelerate as it falls "in order" to hurry home to Mother. The stone moves as it does according to fixed mathematical laws. There are no purposes in nature in the modern imagery of things. There are forces and particles and regularities of happening; but never purposes. As Jacques Monod, the noted French molecular biologist, put it: "The cornerstone of the scientific method is the postulate that nature is objective. In other words, *systematic* denial that 'true' knowledge can be got at by interpreting phenomena in terms of final causes—that is to say, of 'purpose.'"[15]

Galileo was right about the stone, was he not? Can there be serious objection to the systematic elimination of purpose or subjective interiority from the objective universe by modern consciousness? Indeed there can. One of the most vivid such objections was voiced by Theodore Roszak in *The Making of a Counter Culture.* In essence he contends that the deliberate elimination of purpose from the natural world has destroyed human sensitivity to nature and has thereby undermined human sensitivity to the intrinsic independence of the world's being. By rigorously eliminating anthropomorphism from the objective world, the modern vision is left with an absolute gulf between human subjectivity (the In-Here) and everything else (the Out-There). Even other human beings start losing their inwardness before such a consciousness. Roszak writes:

> Now, in fact, anyone, even the most objective scientist, would fall into a state of total paralysis if he *really* believed that

Out-There (beginning with his own organism and unconscious processes) was totally stupid. Nevertheless, In-Here is committed to studying Out-There *as if* it were completely stupid, meaning without intention or wisdom or purposeful pattern. In-Here cannot, if it is to be strictly objective, strive to sympathize in any way with Out-There. It must not attribute to Out-There what cannot be observed, measured, and—ideally—formulated into articulate, demonstrable propositions for experimental verification. In-Here must maintain its alienative dichotomy at all times. And like the racist who cannot under Jim Crow conditions come to see the segregated black man as anything but a doltish and primitive nigger, so In-Here, as the unmoved spectator, cannot feel that Out-There has any ingenuity or dignity. Under this kind of scrutiny, even the other human beings who inhabit Out-There can be made stupid, for they were not made to function within laboratory conditions or according to the exacting needs of questionnaires and surveys. Under the eye of an alien observer they also begin to lose their human purposefulness.[16]

Assuming Galileo to be correct about the stone's fall, is the animal and vegetable world also barren of inwardness or intentions? If we are "objective" in Monod's sense, the question cannot even be taken seriously. Scientistic assumptions rule out the possibility in advance. But from within such a set of assumptions, cultured into a common sense, a consciousness, and a way of life, terrible consequences may follow. One consequence is callous abuse of the natural environment, dismissing any thought of the intrinsic dignity of nonhuman nature and (anthropocentrically!) reducing all thought of purposes in the universe to human purpose. Another is similarly callous abuse of men and women, as well, once they are effectively depersonalized by the habits and values of the objectivistic *mythos.* Torture and mass death, especially when further distanced by impersonal technology, are acts which we recognize, all too painfully, as marks of the modern world.

The high spiritual vision grown out of modern science has led to this, then. The spiritual flaws in objective consciousness have given rise to materialism, overconsumption, obsessive growth, ugliness, ecological crisis, anthropocentric insensitivity to nature, and contempt of human dignity. We stand before an alien universe created, ironically, by the best and most characteristic of our own modern heritage. Let us reflect, then, on the words of Jacques Monod, apostle of the objective consciousness but sensitive to the spiritual costs, the debit side, of modernity. "But there is this too:" he writes, "just as an initial 'choice' in the biological evolution of a species can be binding upon its entire future, so the choice of scientific *practice,* an unconscious choice in the beginning, has launched the evolution of culture on a one-way path; onto a track which nineteenth century scientism saw leading infallibly upward to an empyrean noon hour for mankind, whereas what we see opening before us today is an abyss of darkness."[17]

Many devotees of the modern *mythos* do not yet fear this darkness, however. For them faith in the artificial light of scientific technology is held to be enough to satisfy any spiritual need. Such religious response to technical skill deserves separate attention in the following chapter.

Notes

1. Cited in J. Bronowski, *Science and Human Values* (New York: Harper & Row, 1965), p. 66.

2. Since writing this I have been assured by Professor Priscilla Laws that good scientific work has indeed been done in this personal style, including the work of Rutherford at the turn of this century.

3. Israel Scheffler, *Science and Subjectivity* (Indianapolis: Bobbs-Merrill, 1967), p. 4.

4. Ibid., p. 1.

5. Ibid., p. 5.

6. Ibid.

7. Bronowski, *Science and Human Values,* pp. 66–71.

8. Scheffler, *Science and Subjectivity,* p. 2.

9. Whitehead, *Science and the Modern World,* p. 54.

10. Lewis Mumford, "The Pentagon of Power," *Horizon* 12, no. 4 (1970), p. 10.

11. Cited in E. J. Dijksterhuis, *The Mechanization of the World Picture* (London: Oxford University Press, 1961), p. 362.

12. Michael Polanyi, *Personal Knowledge* (New York: Harper & Row, 1962), pp. 347–358.

13. Barry Commoner, *The Closing Circle: Nature, Man and Technology* (New York: Bantam Books, 1972), p. 73.

14. Ibid., p. 191.

15. Jacques Monod, *Chance and Necessity: An Essay on the Natural Philosophy of Modern Biology* (New York: Vintage Books, 1972), p. 21.

16. Theodore Roszak, *The Making of a Counter Culture* (New York: Doubleday, 1969), pp. 221–222.

17. Monod, *Chance and Necessity,* p. 170.

3. LIMITS OF TECHNOLATRY

Modern science and modern technology are not identical,
though they spring from the same root and share a common
worldview. The imagery of objective consciousness, with its
vision of reality as essentially tangible, measurable,
manipulable, reducible to its smallest parts, empty of intrinsic
ends or values, and amenable to human purpose, is the matrix
for both. Modern technology, however, is the practical
offspring of theoretical science. This distinction does not mark
a sharp separation, of course: modern science as a way of
thinking depends upon the technology of instrumentation,
whereas the demands of technical purpose increasingly shape
the direction of scientific curiosity. But it is still the case that
what makes the technology of the modern world unique is the
power of scientific discovery embodied in the crafts of our
civilization.

Every culture has its arts and crafts, its methods of doing
things. Generally these are handed down by tradition through
apprenticing practices by which crafts of often admirable

sophistication can be attained and preserved. Modern scientific technology, however, operates quite differently: instead of tradition there is deliberate application of explicit natural law; instead of apprenticeship there is research and development.

This shift toward self-conscious, deliberate, highly rationalized ways of doing things is so pervasive in modern culture that the phenomenon deserves a name of its own and has been given one by Jacques Ellul in his now classic study.[1] Ellul calls our characteristically modern way of doing things *technique* and distinguishes it from the methodologies of other cultures by emphasizing the *mode of consciousness* out of which it arises and within which it operates. Ellul acknowledges that methods—ways of doing things—abound, but the field of technique (technical operation) is much more restrictive.

> Two factors enter into the extensive field of technical operation: consciousness and judgment. This double intervention produces what I call the technical phenomenon. What characterizes this double intervention? Essentially, it takes what was previously tentative, unconscious, and spontaneous and brings it into the realm of clear, voluntary, and reasoned concepts.[2]

Ellul's usage has the advantage of broadening the meaning of modern technology beyond its usual designation of hardware. The physical machine remains an important example of technique since machines, to be machines, must be consciously designed and deliberately put to work. The machine, indeed, is our very paradigm of the clearly reasoned way of doing something.[3] It is made in the basic image of technique. But quite evidently the physical machine cannot exhaust the concept. Wherever calculative intelligence intervenes to design a methodology, there is technique. Technique is present in the carefully thought out organization charts of our great corporations; it is present in the scientific methods of breeding and animal husbandry used in our great agricultural industries; it is present in the minutely considered lesson plans and behaviorial objectives employed in our most advanced schoolrooms. The "machine," therefore, need not be made of metal; it may be social or biological or even psychological. Its compelling attractions, in any case, are those underlying technical skill.

I

As I suggested at the end of the previous chapter, technique in this broad sense has become a potent (but frequently unrecognized) religious phenomenon in the modern world. It may be, indeed, that as the conventional religions of our society succumb, by irrelevancy or by surrender, to the implacable currents of scientific-industrial society, the worship of technique is in fact becoming the dominant religious reality of our culture. In any event it will repay us to examine "technolatry" (which is what I shall dub the worship of technique) in any serious effort at contemporary self-understanding.

The vision of technique, functioning as a focus of ultimate religious veneration, is protean and hazardous to represent. Like "God," and "the Kingdom of Heaven," or the like, it is better communicated through the evocative imagery that gives it definiteness than through the lumpish efforts of literal prose. I commend the literature of science fiction[4] and the heady writings of Buckminster Fuller[5] to those who seek such imagery firsthand.

Beyond imagery, however, the worship of technique carries with it certain doctrines that arise out of its imagery; the doctrines, in turn, provoke and reinforce the sense of the sacred that may flow from devoted attention to the images of technique. I shall not attempt a full review of the doctrinal side of technolatry, but at a minimum I should note that technique, as a rational organization of method, presupposes the general metaphysical proposition that the world works always and everywhere by regularities open in principle to human discovery and lawful control. In its ideal form, the image of the machine, supports a *deterministic* vision of the universe: reliable, predictable, intelligible. No unforeseen randomness, balkiness, or ambiguity is permitted in the image of perfect technique. The world of technique is in principle a soluble, a controllable, world.[6]

It is too painfully evident that such a world is not much like our own messy world of daily life[7]—not yet. Like any major religion, technolatry must face and deal with its own "problem of evil." Theodicy, in this case, involves a second major doctrine, this one concerning the nature of history and society. Technique, on this second major doctrine, is inevitably *progressive*. Problems exist, but discoveries will come in time to overcome them all; technical intelligence will not be denied its triumph. Not only so, but the momentum of technique has its own autonomous dynamic.[8] If individual A fails to solve the technical challenge, then individual B, somehow, somewhere, will succeed.

Moreover, for technolatry there is no domain in principle to which the clarifying virtues of technique are not appropriate. The economic and military are exemplar areas for advanced technique, but these are obvious areas for hardware: that is, for technique understood conventionally as technology. Even more pressing requirements for technique exist, so the believer insists, in the political and social areas where rational design has lagged. "In trying to solve the terrifying problems that face us in the world today, we naturally turn to the things we do best," writes B. F. Skinner. "We play from strength, and our strength is science and technology. . . . But things grow steadily worse and it is disheartening to find that technology itself is increasingly at fault."[9] Therefore, Skinner concludes (in a breath-taking inference), "What we need is a technology of behavior."[10] To the devoted technolater every apparent evil brought on by technique is to be countered by yet greater faith in technique. "Though he slay me, yet will I trust in him" (Job 13:15) is a profound religious expression; such is faith's pledge to the sacred.

Doctrine, however, is only the cognitive concomitant of powerful religious experience. Does technique stir the numinous dimension of supreme valuation without which there is no genuine religion, only philosophy and ethics? I affirm that it can and does provoke for many within our culture the sense of sacred mystery best defined by Rudolf Otto in his classic study, *The Idea of the Holy.*[11] The elements of religious experience, Otto showed, are defined by the *mysterium tremendum, timor et fascinans.*

The *mysterium* of religious awe is widely experienced in our culture, when it is experienced at all, thanks to the vast and potent products of scientific technology. I have frequently polled students on this question and have learned to expect that if they report any personal sense of overwhelming mystery, wonder, and creaturely smallness before some unfathomable Other, that Other will have as its characteristic type the thundering magnificence of a Saturn space rocket, the towering grandeur of a modern skyscraper, or the unimaginable violence of a nuclear explosion. It will, in other words, be some incarnation of technique. Even those who feel they understand the workings of some particular technical theophany, moreover, acknowledge the mystery of technique's progressive autonomy as a historical force, above the finite efforts of individual technicians and irreducible to them alone.

The *tremendum,* too, defined by Otto in terms of the tingle of enormous power and sensed dynamic potential, is no less evoked by the images of technique. Thus it is that the *mysterium tremendum* frightens and fascinates at the same time; technique, that is, makes its devotees tremble before it but keeps drawing them back into its awesome embrace.

The *mysterium tremendum, timor et fascinans,* is the essential religious experience. It may be sparked in some societies by a smoking volcano or by images of mythic gods and beasts; it may be stirred in other circumstances by mystic disciplines or by prophetic visions of the righteousness of God; in our society it may be evoked by the ideal of the machine, omnipresent, perfectly designed, infinitely efficient, totally triumphant.

I should not leave the false impression that I suppose great numbers to be constantly in the ecstatic grip of religious fervor, prostrated before some ideal vision of technique. On the contrary, just as there are few ecstatic Christians, even among the many sincere Christian believers left in our modern world, so the sincere devotees of technique in the main hold their faith deeply but untumultuously[12]—except, perhaps, at public celebrations like the "Indianapolis 500" car races and other rituals of its kind.

Tumultuous or not, many of the important values that shape our society, our neighbors, and perhaps ourselves, are those which, drawn out to their fullest degree are the values of technolatry. We are fascinated by devices (of any kind) to get things done (no matter what). The main reason for the popularity of the James Bond films, I suppose, is the fascination we have for the ingenious methods of killing (and of avoiding being killed) that we are treated to in the imagery before us. We endlessly hang upon technique in all domains: in sports, in sex, in business, in politics, in crime, in war. The spirit of technolatry, though usually not heroically manifested, is certainly ubiquitous, and without doubt our society's devotion to technique has borne much fruit. It is time we looked at the quality of these fruits, then, if for any spiritual condition it is true that "by their fruits ye shall know them."

II

I hope I may be excused from dwelling on the marvels that have been wrought by unstinting devotion to technique. We all know the catalogue by heart. Medical technique keeps more of us alive longer than ever before. Agricultural technique gives us more food than the world has ever known. Road-building technique festoons the earth with mighty ribbons of reinforced concrete in an effort to keep ahead of the technique of automobile builders. Aerodynamic technique moves us faster and further. Broadcasting technique fills our minds and shapes our leisure. Sports technique among the professionals has never been so keen. Political technique maintains the system without serious challenge, though with the satisfying entertainment values of apparent conflict and change. Sexual technique multiplies carefully infertile orgasms across the liberated land.

But each marvel, as I list it, brings to any informed mind the sober reminder of an equal and opposite problem. There is a gloomy side even to modern medical technique, not only in the underdeveloped regions of the world where our exported techniques have been directly responsible for the misery of increasingly hopeless growth in population,[13] but also among ourselves where (as Ivan Illich points out) ruinous costs, human indignity, medically caused disease, and degeneration plague our geriatrogenic society.[14] Likewise, scientific agribusiness reaps huge returns, but at a high price in violence toward the land, which may not indefinitely be able to bear the insults of pesticidal, fungicidal, herbicidal, artificially fertilized monocultural technique.[15] I decline even to mention —we know them all—the dark sides of unlimited roadbuilding, of automobile manufacture, of supersonic transport, of videoculture, of sports spectatoritis, of cynical political huckstering, or of empty sexual athleticism. There is something wrong at the root: with unlimited admiration for technique itself. Technolatry, though widespread as a functioning faith in our society is an inadequate religious stance.

Although I respect the potency of technolatry I cannot worship at its shrine. Unlimited adoration of technique is not appropriate, not merely because of particular problems that are currently too obvious, but for more basic reasons that may be summarized in three principles: (1) technique is not *sufficient* for qualitative excellence in any domain of human interest; (2) technique is not even *necessary,* on the whole and beyond an inevitable minimum, for such excellence; and (3) technique carried to excess is *dangerous* in characteristic ways. Let me illustrate these three principles briefly in a familiar nonscientific context and then apply them more generally to our society.

Consider the place of technique in the fine arts. There can be no gainsaying the fact that artistic technique is greatly valued in our culture, and with much reason. There is much more that one can do, in any field of art, if one has developed a high degree of technique. Technical excellence in music, painting, poetry, or the dance, therefore, is the legitimate goal of much hard work in studios and practice rooms wherever the arts are taken seriously. But the principle remains that even the finest technique is not and cannot be the sufficient condition for artistic excellence. The fact has long been recognized. Indeed, one of the earlier uses of the word *technique* in the English language, in *Groves Dictionary of Music* (1884), makes this point quite emphatically: "A player may be perfect in technique, and yet have neither soul nor intelligence."[16]

We all know from personal experience, do we not, that this bleak reminder is correct? Even though we may be unable to define clearly what it is that we find lacking—"musicality," "interpretive sense," "soul," or *je ne sais quoi*—we know that "playing like a clock" will not substitute for "making real music." Just because it defies precision of measurement and articulation, "soul" is outside the reach of technique which, we remember, is by definition a matter of clarity, comprehensibility, and order in the way of doing things. If "soul" cannot be quantified and dissected it cannot be replicated or even recognized by the logic or the language of technique. If there are those who are bothered by my undefined use of the word "soul," I ask them to examine the source of their discomfort: is it due to a tacit supposition that the only significant subjects for thought must be open to precise measurement and clear definition? And on what does this supposition rest? One possibility is that it rests on an unacknowledged faith commitment that insists on overriding even vivid personal intuitions of the indefinable but musically vital quality of "soul." If so, then I ask that a spirit of open empiricism be cultivated since dogmatic closure here against the data of experience begs precisely the question at issue. Another possibility on the other hand is that there are those who have never noticed the differences between "soul" and perfect technique. If so, I hasten on, helpless, to discuss the next principle.

My first principle denies the *sufficiency* of technique for artistic excellence; my second rejects technique's *necessity,* beyond an obvious minimum, as well. In this domain, however, it is difficult to know where this minimum level must be maintained for genuine quality. We must not forget that technique does not mean merely the same things as "method" or "manner," or "style." Clearly, nothing at all can be done in *no* manner or with *no* method. But technique, we recall, comes from the "double intervention" of clarity and calculation against the merely traditional or the spontaneous. To insist on the universal necessity of technique for high artistic quality would be to propose a priori that all primitive or traditional art, whether dances by Bantu tribesmen or paintings by Grandma Moses, be excluded from claims to excellence. Current connoisseurship in the arts would give short shrift to such a sweeping proposal, and in this case I must agree with the connoisseurs. I particularly admire African and Eskimo sculpture. Great skill (as well as "soul") goes into all such excellence, of course, but very little if any technique proper, since these skills and methods are highly traditional and in many cases are far from maximally efficient. Likewise, since "technical" and "spontaneous" are antonyms, the possibility of artistic excellence in improvisation—in jazz or in theatre, in the dance or at the harpsichord—shows still further that ubiquitous technique is not a necessary condition for high achievement.

I do wish immediately, however, to make a significant qualification of this second principle, since otherwise I am sure to be misunderstood. Sheer spontaneity, without any order, clarity, limits, or logic, is not at all likely to result in artistic or any other kind of excellence. I repeat my initial comment: developed technique in the arts is rightly valued for the liberating power that permits us to do much more—even spontaneously—with it than without it. Similarly, the physical instruments of artistic performance, the harpsichords and the saxophones, as well as the skills of the performers, are obviously grounded in sophisticated technique. Thus I wish to affirm that technique *is* needed at *some* level, but I insist that it is neither possible to locate that level with precision nor appropriate to draw it so high as to diminish our appreciation for the traditional or the spontaneous, even sometimes for the unschooled. The musty inefficiencies of tradition and the murky depths of spontaneity (or genius) are equally abhorrent to the clarities of technique, but not the less valuable for all that.

My third principle points up the *dangers* of excessive adulation of technique. In the area of art those dangers show themselves in three significant ways. First, public technolatry in this area of life tends to lead to discouragement and specialization. If Isaac Stern is admired mainly for his incredible technique, and if it is quite clear that only a life dedicated to endless practice (even given the rare talent required) will permit one to rise to such technical heights, then why pick up the fiddle oneself? Better, surely, to turn on the phonograph and let the technique of high fidelity quadruphonic sound carry the professional specialist's awesome technique to one's passive ears. In this way art, music, dance, poetry, drama—even quality conversation— become spectator inactivities, as a culture hypnotized by admiration of unattainable expertise surrenders the creative satisfactions that may rise from lesser technique plus "soul."

A second danger runs close on the heels of the first. Without engagement, creativity, and wrestling with the "soul" of art, even the level of appreciation declines. When admiration is focused too exclusively and too passively on the production of technical effects, the perceived value of what Gray's Dictionary called "soul and intelligence" erodes away; connoisseurship itself atrophies from little use.

Finally, and most seriously of all, perhaps, the technolatrous society, in its latter stages, must spread its values even into the professionalized artistic community itself. Fancy technique becomes the exclusive preoccupation. "Intelligence and soul" are discounted while fads and fashions flash by at an ever accelerating rate, with attention feverishly focused on the "how" rather than the "what," on refinements of technical manner rather than on qualities of artistic matter. Thus the worship of technique leads to the destruction or trivialization of the arts as a humanistic enterprise.

III

Turning now to the modern world of high craft technique, the gist of my argument will be that the same three principles —even the same general sorts of dangers—militate against the fervid adulation of technique as ultimate end. Technique there must be, on these principles, but healthy technique must be freshly integrated into a higher devotion to the art of civilized life.

Will anyone claim that advanced technology is a *sufficient* condition for excellence in human life? If so, let him look around him at the anguish and *anomie* that continues to be evident even in (especially in?) the most highly developed corners of our modern world. That saturation by sophisticated technology in a culture is no guarantee of contentment is becoming a platitude of our times. Sweden, as one of the most uniformly advanced nations in the world, is an instructive example. Quite aside from the often-cited (and sometimes abused) alcohol and suicide statistics, I think of the life work of Ingmar Bergman, cinematic seer of our age, exploring again and again the emptiness of a land without poverty and without God, returning constantly to the search for human substance, for meaning, for . . . "soul." As in the case of music, the *je ne sais quoi* we miss evades precise definition by the logic of technique. Our modern malaise, infecting even those who are most comfortably cocooned by modern gadgetry, is a standing rebuttal to naive hopes that technological achievements, singlehandedly, might be sufficient to assure the full human life.

What, though, of the application of my second principle, implying that, beyond an inevitable minimum, technique is not even a *necessary* condition for the good life? Is high technology actually dispensable? With one major qualification, I argue that this is indeed so. First, ignoring qualifications, it is certainly the case that good and full lives have historically been led without dependence upon what we today think of as technology. It would be insufferable provincialism on our part to maintain the opposite. Engineering technique such as we are discussing is an extremely recent craft launched on the long stream of human history. Anyone whose excellence of life we admire prior to the past few hundred years, at the most, stands as a refutation of the claim that modern engineering technology is in principle a prerequisite for quality in human existence. Even in practice, today, there are those who seek renewed quality in their lives by deliberately turning away from technological society, into the woods or onto the distant islands, in the conviction that life led by tradition or lit by spontaneity will offer more than life ordered by the clarities and efficiencies of technique. As in the case of art, primitivism and improvisation in lifestyle may generate admirable qualities[17] and, however distasteful to the technolatrous consciousness, these alternatives show that high technology, though pervasive, is not in fact as necessary for quality in life as its evangelists may preach.

Here, however, I must introduce my important qualification. Just as in the case of art, I cannot conceive of pure spontaneity or mere tradition bringing about the *best*. High technology is not necessary in principle for the good life; the technological imperative, that is, cannot be mistaken for a

categorical one; but since one can do so much more—since
one is set free into so much grander ranges of creative
possibility—with technique at one's command than without it
(if it is the right sort of chastened technique in the service of
genuine human interests), then it is clearly a necessary
ingredient at some level in aiming at the art of the best in
civilized life. That level is not quantifiable nor precisely
definable, despite the yearnings of technical intellect. It is a
matter of judgment (something that the technical intellect has
been carefully trained to mistrust) rather than of measurement.
But this level of necessity is not only discernible, it is rapidly
rising. If I may put the matter in a quasi-mathematical form,
the level of the necessity of craft technique is directly
proportional to the size of world population and inversely
proportional to the reserves of natural resources. As population
increases and resources dwindle, that is, we are less and less
in a position to look upon advanced technology as an optional
matter. But since the well-meant introduction of technology, as
we have known it hitherto, has been largely responsible for
the demographic dislocations that have filled our world with
unprecedented numbers of persons, and since the availability
of that same technology has been almost wholly responsible
for the unprecedented looting of the earth's treasure, it is
obvious that significant changes of some kind are needed if we
are not to lock ourselves into an ever-tightening graveyard
spiral (as pilots call such vicious circles) that will doom all our
dreams to dust.

I have anticipated in various ways the burden of my third
principle: that technique carried to excess is dangerous. This is
no secret and requires little more comment, perhaps, except to
note some of the analogues between the dangers of
technolatry in the arts and more generally in society. Then, in
the light of all these observations, we will be in a position to
press for certain changes in attitude and practice that will
emerge as needed antidotes in our troubled society.

Fascination by unrestrained technique has led, as we are all aware, to the technologies of large-scale economic centralization. Our admiration of technolatry's cardinal virtue, efficiency, has produced a society dominated by institutions justified by ultimate appeal to efficiencies of scale, no matter how remote they have become from human interests or creative concerns. The literature of our time is rife with discussion of our sensed loss of control, within the "corporate state,"[18] of the economic and political machinery that feeds and clothes, entertains and medicates, transports and taxes, houses and buries us. "The System" is distinct from *us,* the powerless little people who dutifully conform our tastes to what is economic to produce for mass markets. Even the remote managers, like human cogs, feel swept along by the System which they merely serve. Hypnotized by technique, which insinuates its values through multimedia propaganda, then confirms its success by spy and information retrieval, the members of society increasingly experience the passivity of specialization and discouragement before the monolith of unattainable, seemingly omnipotent technical virtuosity. If the psychological analysis of Erich Fromm is right, it is this passivity that lies at the root of modern hopelessness and social pathology.[19] Spectatoritis, not merely in the domains of sport or of the arts, but planted in the soul of society by gigantic and remote technique, is the death of creativity and confidence.

In the second place, analogous to the loss of personal connoisseurship in the arts, the sense of passive alienation from the System leads to a dangerous loss of personal responsibility in society. Every technician is merely doing his job, taking orders, keeping the machinery running. The crucial intuitions of right and wrong are dulled. Within the social machine that is the giant bureaucracy of corporate society— public or private makes no difference—no part need feel personally responsible, even involved. This was the most important moral lesson of the Watergate scandals, through which Americans saw with shattering vividness what their well-bred and educated young social technicians were capable of doing automatically, without compunction or reflection at the time, when the efficient functioning of their intricately designed political machine required it.

Finally, I fear, this fouling of moral connoisseurship combined with the autonomy of the System must lead to destruction of the entire social enterprise. Unlike its analogous danger in the arts, in which excessive emphasis on technique tends to the trivialization and destruction of a humanistic enterprise which contributes just one precious element to the totality of existence, this social danger exists at a level and on a scale which threatens the possibility of civilized life itself. I am concerned, of course, as I indicated in chapter 1, about war, once the autonomous dynamics of rival bureaucracies— each operating efficiently according to its own amoral technological intellect—clash in earnest, armed with the lethal efficiencies of technological armaments. "Advances" in these areas now tend to have a politically destabilizing effect, as the perceived balances of power tilt and sway with shifting technique. The System grinds on, events are in control, and human beings watch helplessly, as it seems to them, from within the belly of Leviathan.

I am no less concerned about self-destructive (and self-delusive) directions in society even in the absence of war, given the continuance of technolatrous faith. One instructive example arises from current biological science. Recently we have been treated to a startling novelty in the history of science: a voluntary self-imposed ban on the application of a powerful scientific technique because of potentially extreme dangers to society. The technique itself permits isolation and rejoining of segments of DNA in such a way that allows the construction of biologically active recombinant DNA molecules in vitro.[20] These molecules can then be stably replicated in *Escherichia coli,* molecular biology's favorite workhorse bacterium which resides—harmlessly, under normal conditions —in the human intestinal tract. The excitement caused by the new technique is of course enormous, both for the theoretical and the practical uses it portends. It seems that the key to real genetic engineering—using hybrid molecules to alter the genetic structure of living organisms at will—is, at last, if not precisely within our grasp, then at least dangling very close to our reach.

Why then the ban? It seems at first glance irrational for scientists to deny themselves bright new tools which promise not only greater understanding of genetic structures but also the realization of such science-fictionlike goals as, for example, inserting nitrogen-fixing genes into plants and thereby ending dependence upon artificial fertilizers once and for all. The problem, however, bluntly put, is plague. This would not be plague in any familiar sense, terrible as that might be, but an unprecedented pandemic raising, as a realistic prospect, the decimation of the entire human race. The basis for this cataclysmic possibility is this same recombinant technique through which may be synthesized entirely new organisms— hybrid organisms, some possibly pathogenic, against which there exist no natural defenses. That is, the widespread application of the new technique cannot but, in the sober words of Paul Berg's Committee on Recombinant DNA Molecules, "result in the creation of novel types of infectious DNA elements whose biological properties cannot be completely predicted in advance."[21] The technique requires *E. coli* bacteria in large numbers. They, in turn, the committee notes, "are capable of exchanging genetic information with other types of bacteria, some of which are pathogenic to man. Thus, new DNA elements introduced into *E. coli* might possibly become widely disseminated among human, bacterial, plant, or animal populations with unpredictable effects."[22]

The Berg Committee, in the context of its unprecedented call for a ban on experiments with the new technique, is perhaps too modest—or insufficiently forthright—in calling the effects it fears "unpredictable." "Incalculable," might have been a better word, since while details might be beyond

prediction, responsible sources are not unable to call a plague
a plague:

> In the worst conceivable case, an *E. coli* bacterium infected by a
> virus which some manipulation had unintentionally rendered
> pathogenic might escape from the laboratory, infect the population
> outside, and set off a human epidemic of perhaps myxomatosis-like
> proportions.[23]

What are the chances, however, of such a "worst case"
accident, with its all-too-foreseeable consequences of race
decimation or suicide? *Science* flatly notes:

> The incidence of laboratory acquired infections—5000 in the last
> 30 years, a third of them in laboratories with special containment
> facilities—suggests that the eventual escape of such an organism, if
> created, could probably be expected.[24]

These, then, were the main reasons for the unprecedented
self-imposition of a total ban on application of this tempting
technique: accidents do happen and must be expected; the
hazards implicit in such an accident are beyond calculation;
therefore the potential gains from use of the technique, though
very great, are not under present circumstances worth the
genocidal possibilities. As the original call for the embargo,
endorsed by the Assembly of Life Science of the National
Research Council of the National Academy of Sciences, put it,
all experiments using the new biological technique should be
stopped "until the potential hazards of such recombinant DNA
molecules have been better evaluated or until adequate
methods are developed for preventing their spread."[25] And to
the credit of the field of molecular biology, the ban was
effectively maintained, as far as is known, all over the world,
pending an international meeting to review the hazards and
make new recommendations.

The story, to this point, counts as a high moment in recent
human history. Automatic adulation of a new technique was
resisted for the sake of broader values. A brilliant technical

development was weighed before it was worshiped. Scientists stepped outside their specialized roles to ponder the wider social good. Interviewed later, Paul Berg is quoted as remarking of the embargo that it is "the first I know of in our field. It is also the first time I know of that anyone has had to stop and think about an experiment in terms of its social impact and potential hazard."[26]

The moment, however, was not to last. In February, 1975, an international conference, called by Berg's organizing committee, met at the Asilomar conference center near Monterey, California, with technique again irresistibly in the ascendancy. No new information lessening the probable biohazard, no new controls against the spread of man-made pathogens, had become available in the months between July and February; but the pressures to use the new techniques had become unbearable. As *Science* succinctly summarized:

> Few scientists acquainted with the power of the new technique would lightly forgo its use, yet how could the public be informed the moratorium was at an end when the unknown hazards that caused it to be invoked in the first place were just as unknown as before?[27]

Nothing objective, that is, had changed in the situation of the scientists vis-à-vis the human race. But any strong temptation, stared at long (and longingly) enough, can work wonders in changing subjective perceptions of costs and benefits. Thus, after three and one half days of debate over alternative means of doing so, the Asilomar conference, by consensus, lifted the historic embargo on experimentation with recombinant DNA molecules, substituting pious promises (to be very careful) for their new onerous pledges of total abstinence.

Where does this leave us? It is possible, of course, that in this specific case society will impose, in self-defense, a ban on what technologically dazzled specialists cannot bring themselves voluntarily to forgo. It is possible, too, that the human race will be lucky for a long time. All of us can hope that the fatal genie, once created by technique, will be kept well stoppered by technique. But, willy-nilly, it is in technique, this group of biologists has decided for us, that we must now put our ultimate trust.

This is merely one example from among a host of possible ones in which our fascination by technique draws us into perils against which we pose defenses based mainly on faith in still more technique. But this is no coincidence. It is the historic fruit of long-nourished priorities. Our society's primary problem is in learning to do regularly and in sustained ways what molecular biologists, in a spasm of conscientious scruple, did briefly: in Paul Berg's fateful words, to "stop and think."

Another, more widely debated example of the need to "stop and think" is the inexorable march of decisions leading toward more and more reliance on nuclear fission as our society's primary source of energy. Despite warnings from such farseeing experts as Professor Paul S. Lykoudis, in testimony given to the United States government,[28] of dangers from thermal pollution, and (given fast-breeder reactors) incredibly toxic plutonium, high energy densities in the core, widespread bomb potential, and unsolved (perhaps insoluble) storage and waste problems, still work goes on apace toward the technical goal of shifting our society onto nuclear fission. Even Professor Lykoudis supports such efforts, though as "only an intermediate step" toward fusion and solar energy sources. The feeling of fate, the sense of the technological imperative as somehow categorical, the presumption of autonomy for the System, looms very strong. And yet we must not avert our eyes to what this direction, if continued, might mean to us and to our children. Plutonium, once created by technique, cannot be destroyed by known technique. As far as can be seen with confidence today, only time, time measured in many thousands of years,[29] not by historical but by geological scales, will reduce the intensity of these immensely toxic radioactive materials. Even as we intend "only an intermediate step"[30] to tide us over (if everything goes well) to a more benign

technique, we are in fact planning to produce on a large scale
lethal poisons and potential explosives for all significant time to
come, but without any presently assured method of keeping
them safe from future mishap. Earthquakes, wars, highjackings,
whole civilizations, will come and go while the wastes from
our "intermediate step" continue—for all we now can
reasonably see—to threaten any exposed organic life and thus
to pose a grisly reminder to our descendants, if such there be,
through all future history, of our momentary economic
desperation with its permanent consequences. I for one bewail
the prospect of being a member of the supremely heedless—
some would say criminal[31]—generation, in all likelihood to be
remembered in infamy forever for what we are amorally
planning and rationally working so hard to achieve in the next
few decades.

IV

Our sense of helplessness before the seemingly autonomous
system as it continues to accelerate its mad rationality toward
ruin must not be allowed to sap our courage to define, and
press for, new direction. This will mean the nurturing of new
consciousness in ourselves as we, personally, awaken all too
fitfully and dimly to our situation; it will mean cultivating
intuitions of humanity, of qualitative dimensions in experience,
of "soul," or of "the things that matter in life." It will mean
rejecting the deeply ingrained assumption from the time of
Galileo and Descartes that what counts is the countable and
only the countable. It will mean thinking, and courageously
urging others to think, some hitherto unthinkable thoughts; it
will mean sometimes trusting holistic judgment above
calculations of demonstrable short-term utility; it will mean
reorganizing our lives and our careers according to the
precepts of a deeper spiritual wisdom than the too easily
marketable doctrines of technolatry.

Specifically, moving our selves and our society beyond
technolatry will require the spiritual strengths of prophetic

prohibition and priestly redirection within the numinous domain of technique. There are times, as the great Hebrew prophets knew, to say a firm NO to temptation. Compromise is sometimes sin. One such time, I submit, is our present situation regarding experimentation with recombinant DNA molecules. Another is at the point of large-scale development and use of plutonium-breeding nuclear reactors without known, reliable, and feasible methods for dealing with their long-term dangers.

The consequences to our energy-hungry economy and to our hyperconsuming way of life may be severe, I recognize, if we voluntarily deny ourselves the energy wealth that fast breeder technique, heedless of the future, could probably supply.[32] Even those economic perils might be somewhat averted, of course. On the basis of a firm and *early* moral decision, for posterity's sake, to resist the temptations of such technique, we might vastly multiply our efforts to shift our economy from oil to humble coal and wind and tide and even wood as our intermediate steps toward fusion and solar energy. And our efforts, complete with frugal consumption, might see us through. But even if it should mean permitting economic collapse and chaos for a painful but relatively short time, historically speaking, there are some things that are too terrible to do even in the defense of our accustomed affluent way of life, are there not? If the answer given should be no— that literally anything technologically feasible is to be grasped, no matter what the long-term consequences, no matter how unforeseeable or uncontrollable the evils that might be anticipated to flow from such technique—then blind technolatrous commitment is giving reply, not morally considered human judgment.

On the other hand, it has long been part of the priestly tradition to redirect spiritual energies, including possibly destructive ones, into the service of legitimate spiritual ends. Here, I think, is where the main work needs to be done by those in a position to give new shape to the dynamics of technique in our time and for the future. I have already argued that the level of necessity for technology is high and growing higher. The problem then posed was that unless important changes in technological impact are made, our current graveyard spiral toward destruction may well be tightened and accelerated. Creative engineering, liberated from the narrow imperatives of technolatry, is urgently needed to proceed with those important changes. In an airplane, the way out of a graveyard spiral is to loosen the controls, ease up on the throttle, gently roll in opposite aileron and rudder, then level off at a safe altitude. It is not an antitechnological maneuver but a significant (life-enhancing) change in the way the technological controls are set. In this sense, the Gould, Inc., slogan, "Science and technology must answer our problems. If they don't, nothing else will,"[33] is correct. But it must not be interpreted to mean more technology of the same sort. A new and gentler, more humane technology is in order.

Specifically, to continue the example from nuclear engineering, I would urge responsible and concerned professionals to devote vastly greater effort to the solution of the nuclear wastes problem. Our whole modernized society, worldwide, seems hellbent on tying its future energy demand (which somehow cannot even be conceived by official spokesmen as stabilizing, much less diminishing) to nuclear fission, whether *or not* the clear dangers of bombs by theft or ecocide by leakage are securely prevented in advance. My argument is that the engineering profession ought not to pander to society's passion for energy, especially with fast breeder reactors, unless and until our responsibility to the next thousand generations has been clearly, demonstrably, reliably met *first*. Technolatrous daydreams about past engineering triumphs are no substitute; vague hopes and blind faith that "something will turn up" are no solution. Above all, the irresponsible readiness to let some other engineers (or some other generation) cope with the lethal leavings of our affluence is monstrous. Therefore, since worldwide moral restraint cannot safely be assumed in this imperfect world, there is no more important project for engineers who are aware of the historic stakes than the development of a defense against the threat of plutonium and other long-lived radioactive products. Call it Project Posterity, if you like, and let it produce—in the time available—the needed hardware for transmutation techniques, for disposal into outer space (or into the sun), or at worst, for guaranteed million-year leak-proof containers. Project Posterity will also be challenged to design all the techniques of handling, transport, and storage that will have to be fail-safe against sabotage and impervious to geological convulsions or other "acts of God." In all of this, Project Posterity must plan for service-free safety beyond the lifetime of our civilization, or its successor's successor. What a challenge Project Posterity poses! Perhaps it will be the most difficult engineering project ever undertaken by mankind. But the world needs it, in the long run, more than it needs fission power itself. Without it, large-scale fission power should not be set loose upon the earth. Project Posterity would in truth be engineering for life; it would be one example of technique in the service of "soul."

A number of other writers have attempted to describe the outlines of widely applied technique of this sort. Ivan Illich calls for "convivial" tools, designed to help the little, currently powerless (and passive) person express his or her own individuality and experience his or her own creative potential in industries of comprehensible scale.[34] E. F. Schumacher now uses the term "appropriate" technology to describe the modest, life-enhancing, miniaturized technique that he recommends not only for developing countries but also to add richness of texture and balance to the economics of developed ones seeking the more important things in life.[35] Aldous Huxley emphasized the virtues in decentralization of the megaindustrial world, with special attention to the need for working toward local self-sufficiency in food and in energy supplies.[36] Consider the creative challenge to engineering, if

Huxley's call should be heeded! What potential energy sources are relatively evenly spread around the world? How can these be efficiently harnessed for relatively cheap, environmentally acceptable, local production? Can fusion reactors be miniaturized? Here is a job to keep nuclear engineers engrossed for generations. Meanwhile, how shall adequate supplies of solar or wind energy be stored[37] when the sun is not shining or the wind blowing? The political and human liberation that would flow from the successful practical answering of such questions staggers the imagination. The current System would not happily adjust to our freedom from the sheiks of Arabia and Texas, or to the withering away of the Grid; but people have been forced too long into automatic adjustment to the System of energy and other standardized monopolies ruled from afar. With creative engineering and a newly humanized technology, perhaps the System will be required to adjust to human scale, for a change.

What a gigantic change, though, this adjustment would symbolize! It would necessarily represent the "resecularizing" of technique, the turning of the idol into a tool once more. To hope for such a transformation would be to hope for a new post-modern form of consciousness, beyond technolatry, that would experience fresh value priorities and would see the world in deeply different ways. Failing such an adjustment, on the other hand, I foresee collapse, as I have argued in chapters 1 and 2, due to dynamic flaws implicit in the System of the modern world itself. In either event, adjustment or collapse, the end of naïve modern consciousness as we have known it seems highly probable. The time has come, therefore, to speculate a bit on what post-modern consciousness may turn out to be, and to clarify our preferences while there is still time to throw our influence into the balance for the future we might choose.

Notes

1. Jacques Ellul, *The Technological Society,* trans. John Wilkinson (New York: Vintage Books, 1964.

2. Ibid., p. 21.

3. *See* for delightful discussions of this theme, Robert M. Pirsig, *Zen and the Art of Motorcycle Maintenance: An Inquiry into Values* (New York: William Morrow, 1974).

4. *See,* for example, the works of Arthur C. Clarke; e.g., *The City and the Stars* (New York: Harcourt, Brace and World, 1953).

5. A good sample of stirring "mental mouthfuls and ventilated prose" can be found in R. Buckminster Fuller, *No More Secondhand God* (Garden City, N.Y.: Anchor Books, 1971).

6. In Clarke's *The City and the Stars,* he introduces the ingenious device of the character Khedron, the Jester, whose function in the totally planned, "perfect" technological city, Diaspar, is to introduce a limited amount of instability through his (officially sanctioned) pranks. "Let us say that I introduce calculated amounts of disorder into the city," he says. Thus even randomness is programmed, in judicious amounts, into the Central Computer, as a prophylactic against the decadence of excessive stability—even chaos is subordinated to technical control.

7. For arguments opposing the doctrinaire determinist conception of our world, *see* my "Self-Determinism," *American Philosophical Quarterly* 10, no. 3 (July 1973), pp. 165–176.

8. Ellul, *The Technological Society,* p. xxviii.

9. B. F. Skinner, *Beyond Freedom and Dignity* (New York: Bantam Books, 1971), p. 1.

10. Ibid., p. 3.

11. Rudolf Otto, *The Idea of the Holy,* 2nd ed., trans. John W. Harvey (New York: Oxford University Press, 1950).

12. For a fuller discussion of the contrast between ideal and actual religion, *see* my *Basic Modern Philosophy of Religion,* p. 70 ff.

13. *See* Ansley J. Coale, "The History of the Human Population,"

Scientific American 231, no. 3 (September 1974), pp. 41–51. *See also* Paul Demeny, "The Populations of the Underdeveloped Countries," ibid., pp. 149–159.

14. Ivan Illich, *Tools for Conviviality* (New York: Harper & Row, 1973), esp. chap. 1.

15. Thomas W. Wilson, Jr., *World Food: The Political Dimension* (Washington, D.C.: The Aspen Institute, 1974), chap. 3. *See also* Barry Commoner, *The Closing Circle,* chap. 5.

16. *The Oxford English Dictionary* (New York: Oxford University Press, 1971).

17. This is the guiding principle behind the Outward Bound program, which has been reported on ecstatically by several of my students who have tried and survived its rigors. For a discussion from the viewpoint of American literature of the rhythms of withdrawal to primitive nature for sustenance, *see* Leo Marx, "Pastoral Ideals and City Troubles," *Western Man and Environmental Ethics: Attitudes Toward Nature and Technology,* ed. Ian G. Barbour (Reading, Mass.: Addison-Wesley, 1973), pp. 93–115.

18. Charles A. Reich, in *The Greening of America* (New York: Random House, 1970), coined this term to designate the amalgam of "public" and "private" bigness in ruling our lives. Herbert Marcuse offers a similar critique from a different temperamental and philosophical standpoint in *One-Dimensional Man* (Boston: Beacon Press, 1964). The literature beyond these is extensive.

19. Erich Fromm, *The Revolution of Hope: Toward a Humanized Technology* New York: Bantam Books, 1968).

20. *See* Paul Berg et al., "Potential Biohazards of Recombinant DNA Molecules," *Science* 185 (26 July 1974), p. 303.

21. Ibid., p. 303.

22. Ibid.

23. *Science* 187 (14 March 1975), p. 932.

24. Ibid.

25. Berg et al., "Potential Biohazards," p. 303.

26. *Science* 185 (26 July 1974), p. 332.

27. *Science* 187 (14 March 1975), p. 932.

28. Paul S. Lykoudis, "The Role of Nuclear Power and Advanced Energy Systems in the United States," given in testimony at Project Independence hearings in Chicago, September 1974.

29. The half-life of most of the plutonium created in the fast-breeder

reactor is approximately 25,000 years; but since this means that only *half* the dangerous radioactivity of this substance has disappeared in that length of time—time equivalent to all of history and much of human prehistory (back to neolithic man)—the dimensions of this real problem are much greater yet. Little wonder, then, that some experts speak in terms of having to cope with a *million*-year problem, as did Glen Seaborg, former chairman of the Atomic Energy Commission, in a lecture at Purdue University, 18 February 1975.

30. Lykoudis, "The Role of Nuclear Power," p. 2.

31. E. F. Schumacher, *Small is Beautiful: Economics as if People Mattered* (New York: Harper Torchbooks, 1973), p. 137, writes: "To do such a thing is a transgression against life itself, a transgression infinitely more serious than any crime ever perpetrated by man. The idea that a civilization could sustain itself on the basis of such a transgression is an ethical, spiritual, and metaphysical monstrosity."

32. I say "probably" because the certainty of success is by no means presently agreed. Even Dr. Edward Teller, high priest of technology, has his doubts—not about the *morality* but the feasibility of the fast breeder—as he told the Worcester Polytechnic Institute: "I used to think this was a really important project . . . but, we've been trying to get it going for twenty-nine years and it hasn't worked yet. I think there's a lesson there." "How Technology Can Solve the Problem," reprinted from *The WPI Journal* (August 1974) in *Skeptic* (Special Issue no. 5), p. 54.

33. *Technology: Abandon, endure or advance?* (Chicago: Gould, Inc., n.d.), p. 12. This slogan comes at the end of each of Gould, Inc.'s series of pamphlets on the subject, available from 8550 W. Bryn Mawr Ave., Chicago, Ill. 60631.

34. Illich, *Tools for Conviviality.*

35. Schumacher, *Small is Beautiful.*

36. Aldous Huxley, *Science, Liberty and Peace* (New York: Harper & Bros., 1946).

37. Huxley stressed the key importance of designing a really good battery nearly thirty years ago when he wrote: "One of the most urgent tasks before applied science is the development of some portable source of power to replace petroleum—a most undesirable fuel from the political point of view, since deposits of it are rare and unevenly distributed over the earth's surface, thus constituting natural monopolies which, when in the hands of strong nations, are used to

increase their strength at the expense of their neighbors and, when possessed by weak ones, are coveted by the strong and constitute almost irresistible temptations to imperialism and war. From the political and human point of view, the most desirable substitute for petroleum would be an efficient battery for storing the electric power produced by water, wind or the sun." (Ibid., p. 82.)

II

THE SEARCH FOR A POST-MODERN CONSCIOUSNESS

4. RETURN OF MAGIC

The next three chapters of this book will be aimed at stimulating some needed thought about possible religious successors for modern technolatry in a desirable post-modern world. This topic could become a bog. Therefore I shall impose two limits on my speculations.

The first limit reflects the political slogan: "You can't beat somebody with nobody." As Thomas Kuhn notes, regarding revolutionary shifts in the history of scientific thought, "crises of confidence" in fundamental paradigms never by themselves result in radical change until "an alternative candidate is available to take its place."[1] The same principle is true, I suggest, with regard to the even deeper mythic paradigms of consciousness that concern us here. Modern consciousness and its attendant technolatry is currently suffering strong shocks from without and crumbling of confidence from within. But the transition to post-modernity will not happen without some alternative "candidate," as Kuhn puts it, standing ready. If so, it will be prudent to remain alert to what is actually available today. Perhaps, just as scientific consciousness gestated in the matrix of Christian world-images before the modern world was born, so somewhere in the world around us now we may find a precursor of the dominant consciousness of the post-modern world that is on its way.

My second self-limitation is based on the conviction that Western peoples, generally, are not likely to adopt modes of consciousness that are not already rooted deeply within Western tradition. Not all the modern world is Western, of course; the Japanese, for example, may have different post-modern alternatives available to them than do Germans or Americans. But since these short chapters can make no pretense of comprehensiveness, only suggestiveness, I have chosen to focus on the Western heritage that I and most of my readers know best.

Are there, then, within that heritage, actual candidates for consciousness that might let us hope for a better post-modern world? Whatever they are, if they are to improve upon the flaws we have noted in modern consciousness, they will need to give promise of grounding social attitudes far more intimately attuned to nature's needs than our present form of consciousness has done. They will need to promise to leave behind the controlling, progressive, prideful postures of technolatrous conquest and exploitation. They will doubtless also be based on a world-image far different from that of objective consciousness. What might some of these candidates be?

I

There is an underculture, or as Theodore Roszak named it, a counterculture, ready to claim the role of successor to the modern culture when it passes out of history's limelight. What is especially noteworthy about this counterculture (not by any means limited to the young, or the "hip" of the late 1960s, or the users of drugs) is its characteristic belief in the occult, the magical, the mystical, and the strange. I propose to take this return to magical consciousness seriously in our search for a mythic matrix for a livable post-modern world.

In the first place, the resurgence is an interesting social phenomenon. Occultism seems to be a permanent feature of Western civilization, rising from time to time into prominence as it did in the early 1970s. That rise, despite all the triumphs of objective modern consciousness, was as startling as it was significant. Who could have predicted it? Certainly not I, at least, despite much contact with bright and "with-it" young people in my classes during the late 1950s and early 1960s. In those years we were wrestling, in philosophy and religion, with the possibility of *any* responsible belief that did not have the direct sanction of science. Objective consciousness, as it had been since the seventeenth century, was on the offensive against credulity of all sorts, including the suspected credulity even of distinguished theological scholars. It was avant garde to be critical; scientific skepticism still had a youthful feel. Only the old and stodgy had a timidly kind word for the possibility of the supernatural of any sort, however abstract and sanitized. No one ever expressed interest in or sympathy for astrology—much less witchcraft and magic. Such blatant superstition was never even considered in my circles, though I knew that some credulous people must be requiring the newspapers to keep printing those silly horoscopes.

How things changed! One of the vivid moments of truth about the change hit me in—of all places—Los Alamos, New Mexico, at the beginning of the 1970s. Los Alamos is a most unusual town, sometimes called "Atom City, U.S.A.," because of its significant scientific and technical contributions. Built by the United States government and populated with top-quality physicists and engineers, the city is still practically all made up of scientists or science support workers. I expected (and found, among the adults) a bastion of objective consciousness, a veritable Vatican City of modernity. Imagine my astonishment, then, to be introduced at the Los Alamos High

School, where I was serving as a consultant in humanities, and immediately to be plunged into serious and prolonged discussion with a large group of students on witchcraft! As a philosopher of religion I was someone they felt they could talk to about their interests and concerns. Almost all the students professed to believe in magic. It was merely distinguishing black from white magic that disturbed them. One young woman professed herself a witch and others soberly agreed.

Moving back and forth between that youth world and the parental world of cyclotrons and lasers (the superintendent of schools met me in his laboratory in his white coat and gave me a fascinating tour of *his* magic) was an unforgettable experience for me. Witches in Los Alamos! Afterward, as I flew my Cessna over the rugged New Mexican terrain and watched the sparsely settled Indian country slide beneath me, I felt the gap again, between my airborne technological cocoon and the lands of rain dance and shamanistic flight. Did Don Juan teach Castaneda to fly without all this technology? Are there "separate realities" to learn from the Yaqui way of knowledge?[2]

Since then the craze for the occult has receded somewhat. It became faddish and, as one might expect in the modern world, commercialized. But the blossoming again of occult fascination even in late modern times was a portentous reminder of a very real "candidate" not far off center stage.

Nor was all of this occult outbreak merely passing fad. Some of it remains exceedingly interesting. What on earth can we make of acupuncture? How can we cope with reports about extrasensory perception, telepathy, the photographing of bodily auras, psychokinesis at Stanford University, and all the results in these areas being claimed in the Soviet Union and elsewhere in Eastern Europe?[3] How shall we respond to the recent crowd of books on Atlantis and on evidence of early space visitations to the earth? Speaking of space events, are we quite sure about the status of unidentified flying objects? Is there nothing at all to the UFO's? And, back to earth, how

shall we deal with the spate of strange reports that our
vegetable environment is not only alive but aware?[4]

There are important implications for post-modern
consciousness in these questions. The first of these implications
is that a great deal of resistance to *noticing* possible data is
being broken down. Thanks to the outbreak of the occult, our
possibilities for experience are being expanded.

For modern objective consciousness all this is strictly
nondata. It simply cannot be data; it fails to fit with what can
be contained in the objective world-image; there must be
something wrong with allegations and reports citing such
things. Acupuncture, for example, has no basis in physiological
theory nor in modern scientific medicine. No nervous system
parallels the points on the body where those little needles are
inserted and twirled; no known or imaginable bodily
mechanism could kill pain or cure illness through such
treatment. It *must* be fakery; its practice is rooted in ancient
Chinese lore about spiritual points of power, and all that. How
could it be anything but flimflam abetted by foolishness? And
yet James Reston, internationally known columnist, reports that
it worked on him when suddenly needing emergency surgery
in China. And yet one of my former students—someone I
would trust with my life to tell the truth—experienced cure in
China immediately after treatment with the little gold needles.
And Americans watched during the Nixon visit to China while
their television sets showed surgery and childbirth aided by
acupuncture—one woman was even interviewed during
surgery with no anesthetic but the rotating needles. But still
most of us refuse to believe it. How can this be data? Don't
bother to think about it—there's got to be something wrong
somewhere!

Mental telepathy is just as bad. Objective consciousness
refuses to acknowledge the data as data. There is no way ESP
could happen in the objective world picture. No possible
mechanism could account for what is claimed by researchers
like Rhine at Duke University and all the rest.[5] I recall an
evening-long debate some years ago between H. H. Price, the

distinguished Oxford philosopher who was then president of the British Society for Psychical Research, and a professor in the psychology department at a university where I then taught. We were in the psychologist's living room, and metaphorically this was appropriate since he never once left his familiar mental furniture, despite the wealth of reports of investigated incidents he was offered by Professor Price. The proferred data were nondata to the psychologist. Once admitted they would not be able to fit the scientistic image of the world. Therefore they could not be admitted.

I encountered the same reaction, from a computer specialist this time, concerning *The Secret Life of Plants*. What a scornful rejection of any possibility that mere plants without nervous systems could feel or be aware or respond to emotional conditions in their surroundings! Ludicrous! A scandalous manipulation of the evidence! Had my critical friend read the book? What's the point? There's no use wasting time over such nonsense.

In this way, and many others like it, the world-picture of objective consciousness had closed the doors of perception against the deeply inexplicable, which is what the occult basically means. Not the merely puzzling, which objective consciousness allows and even revels in, but the deeply— threateningly—inexplicable is what is not admitted to consciousness, often literally not seen. Many recent experiments in perception, such as those famous ones by J. S. Bruner and Leo Postman,[6] have shown that it is difficult and disconcerting, at best, to see what is incongruous with one's categories of normal expectation. The objective world-picture which we reviewed in chapter 2 provides for objective modern consciousness just those basic categories of normal expectation. And to the extent that expectation channels perception, the world-picture of modern consciousness has acted as blinders on experience, keeping the gaze from wandering disturbingly far either to left or right of the well-worn path.

One positive implication of the new outbreak of interest in

the occult, therefore, is the assistance it has given in expanding possibilities of experience itself. It has constituted a creative disturbance, at the very least, to the complacency of modern consciousness. From the point of view of genuine science (though not that of scientism) these results should be regarded as valuable, since openness and humility before the data is one of objective consciousness's primary values. From a scientific point of view, this new openness to possible data will give researchers for the first time a chance to take seriously enough to *test* which of these data are reliable. From a philosophical point of view, one still less wedded to the scientistic world-picture, this implication of recent developments is even more cheerfully to be welcomed.

But before modern consciousness lowers its guard before this first implication, we had better note a second. Even the act of taking seriously the *possibility* of data surrounding the occult reflects a significant change in consciousness itself. It shows a major erosion in the confidence of modern mentality and a transition toward something unmistakably post-modern.

Consider the implications, for example, of taking astrology seriously—even to the extent of searching for data. A friend of mine in Philadelphia publishes a book largely devoted to methods of astrological birth control.[7] I have asked him to send me data that would compare astrological methods with other, characteristically modern, methods of limiting families and determining the sexes of children. But what am I asking? I am guilty of urging him to combine two utterly incompatible world-images.

Astrology has a long history, much longer that that of the modern world. It assumes a wholly different vision of the universe, best systematized by Ptolemy who wrote in his *Almagest* not only the authoritative astronomical text that lasted until Copernicus and Galileo, but also the definitive astrological work of the ancient and medieval world. Ptolemy's image of things shows earth and man at the center of things, with the fateful stars and planets surrounding the human sphere with their mysterious influences. The universe as a whole is unified by meanings being emanated, being discovered, working themselves out. Man is terribly small and weak, but terribly important, too, in the scheme of things. Everything fits, everything matters. Great events are foretold in the stars; small children inherit their characters from the heavenly conjunctions under which they are born.

The Renaissance period was another time of astrological resurgence. Renaissance humanism is usually thought of as a movement of liberation, and, indeed, astrology was not typically seen by the Renaissance as imposing impersonal fate on mankind but, quite the reverse, as a symbol of the humanization of the universe. The early scientist, Roger Bacon, was often cited in the Renaissance for his proastrological views. As Eugenio Garin, the historian of science, says of Bacon: "In his view all relations were ultimately personal relations rather than numbers and measures and causes."[8]

But what a radically different, uncompromisable perspective modern consciousness requires! Either the stars are vastly distant nuclear furnaces formed at random and positioned by blind gravitational forces—in which case they can obviously have no significance for human events or human character—or they stand in some intimate, meaningful relation to the lives of recently evolved two-legged creatures spinning about on the third planet of one of the stars near the edge of the Milky Way Galaxy. No, wait! That last alternative is obviously an impossible, mongrelized one. Astrology as a value-laden, humanizing image of the world fits the Ptolemaic astronomical picture, but if we are to take the modern astronomical vision for fact, the absurdities begin to mount. How would the fate foretold by a red giant star compare with a white dwarf? Are there astral meanings emanating from black holes, into which all else is failing? Does being born under a quasar make you queasy?

Compromise is beyond conceiving. Either the modern world-picture is wrong at its very core about what the stars are, how they originated, how they move and interact, and what our rather peripheral place is in the whole vast universe, or astrology is totally unfounded. There is no having it both ways. And we should note, to raise the stakes even higher, that if we reject modern astronomy we must abandon not only that one science but also physics and chemistry and the whole modern worldview. Are we still willing to keep an open mind about possible data? Are there to be no limits to credulity in post-modern consciousness?

One more example, before we further weigh the strengths and weaknesses of the magical consciousness, calls for brief notice—perhaps because I am more attracted to it than to astrology. Consider the implications of being open to the data alleged by the authors of *The Secret Life of Plants.* My computer specialist friend had much provocation for his scorn. To take seriously these recent claims about the possible awareness by plants of our emotional states requires us to suspend judgment about such other "scandals" as telepathy (how else can plants know our moods, without sense organs?) and even about the nature of life and mind. What is mind? The objective consciousness, as we saw in chapter 2, has always been skittish about the question. But typically, where recognized at all, it has been considered a phenomenon of highly developed nervous systems. If plants have minds but no nervous systems, what are the implications for *our* minds? If there are effective realities other than, but operating on, the physical universe, what will happen to our vision of reality? To take these matters seriously, then, requires a nearly total shift away from the familiar consciousness of modernity and—besides—would force us at the outset to reorder, in possibility at least, our view of the vegetable world surrounding us.

The obstacles to compromise with objective consciousness, though less blatant than in the case of astrology, are still very sharp. Besides the radical shift in world-picture that would be required, one's experimental methodology could not remain unchanged. As stressed in *The Secret Life of Plants,* these experiments cannot be approached in a cool, disinterested, impersonal way. The experimenter must acknowledge his subjectivity and treat it as one essential ingredient in the total outcome. A domineering or unfeeling, controlling attitude will cause the plants to withdraw, "go dead," refuse to cooperate. They must be loved—or at least be given genuine approval—before they will give in return. But this threatens the root of objective consciousness. To give up impersonality of approach would not be to compromise in hopes of finding data, it would be to profane the sacred value, to treat with the devil of credulity, to enter apostasy.

"So be it, then!" say some. Perhaps. But let us not suppose that these are minor adjustments. These are changes requiring a complete recasting of the modern world-picture and a radical surrender of the modern devotion to objectivity. Let us now assess the occult consciousness, supposing that this may be a genuine candidate for the mythic matrix of the post-modern world.

II

One of the most striking points in favor of magical consciousness is surely the enriching effect it must have on personal experience. I was too restrained earlier when I remarked on the benefits of increased noticing—of taking the blinders off—from (even) the scientist's point of view. Then I spoke merely of having access to a wider range of potential data, and that is true as far as it goes; but how much more needs to be said! For magical consciousness the world comes alive—really alive, with an interior being and meaning and purposes all its own—for the first time. Theodore Roszak writes eloquently of the "eyes of fire" that will see more vividly and more truly. The shaman typifies Roszak's sense of what magic should mean to post-modern men:

> Magic, as the shaman practices it, is a matter of communing with the forces of nature as if they were mindful, intentional

presences, as if they possessed a will that requires coaxing, argument, imprecation. When he conjures, divines, or casts spells, the shaman is addressing these presences as one addresses a person, playing the relationship by ear, watching out for the other's moods, passions, attitudes—but always respectful of the other's dignity. For the shaman, the world is a place alive with mighty, invisible personalities; these have their own purposes, which, like those of any person, are apt to be ultimately mysterious. The shaman is on intimate terms with the presences he addresses; he strives to find out their ways and move with the grain of them. He speaks of them as "you," not "it."[9]

The shaman, then, is one who knows that there is more to be seen of reality than the waking eye sees. Besides our eyes of flesh, there are eyes of fire that burn through the ordinariness of the world and perceive wonders and terrors beyond. In the superconsciousness of the shaman, nothing is simply a dead object, a stupid creature; rather, all the things of the earth are swayed by sacred meanings.[10]

What a different way of seeing the world this would be! How much richer than the deracinated experience of modern consciousness, isolated by anthropocentric smugness from an alien universe! I have tasted a small sample of the difference, lately, when, after reading *The Secret Life of Plants,* I looked with new eyes at the faithful old philodendron on my office window sill. "Perhaps you are a sentient being, my good old green friend. Certainly you are not mere office decor, like the other familiar objects on the window sill. Long life to you, and happiness, too!"

A second strength of such consciousness, besides the intrinsic good of enriched daily experience, would be the restoration of what Jacques Monod has called the broken covenant between man and nature. Monod, the molecular biologist, even considers the possibility that our human need for such a "covenant" may be genetic and inborn. "If it is true," he speculates, "that the need for a complete explanation is innate, that its absence begets a profound ache within; if the only form of explanation capable of putting the soul at ease is that of a total history which discloses the meaning of man by assigning him a necessary place in nature's scheme; if to appear genuine, meaningful, soothing, the 'explanation' must blend into the long animist tradition, then we understand why it took so many thousands of years for the kingdom of ideas to be invaded by the one according to which objective knowledge is the *only* authentic source of truth."[11] And, I may add, then we understand the great appeal of the occult, which, as we saw in connection with Renaissance astrology, "rehumanizes" the universe. Mankind, for occult consciousness, is not alone in an alien universe. There are other intelligences, evil and good, which surround, enrich, and limit human life. The need for seeing and feeling the universe a *home* again, then, is a second recommendation of magical consciousness for post-modern civilization.

The third recommendation is practical. We have seen the possible consequences of objective consciousness in ravaging the earth in the absence of any ground for moral limit on human exploitation of a "disqualified" nature. Magical consciousness, however, would call halt to what must eventually end anyway, by human restraint or by environmental collapse. It is practically most vital, therefore, to have a vision of nature that will supply motives for restraint and harmony in place of modern attitudes of excess and conquest. Here are the words of a California shaman:

> The white people never cared for land or deer or bear. When we Indians kill meat, we eat it all up. When we dig roots, we make little holes. . . . We shake down acorns and pine-nuts. We don't chop down the tress, kill everything. The tree says, "Don't. I am sore. Don't hurt me." But they chop it down and cut it up. The spirit of the land hates them. . . . The Indians never hurt anything, but the white people destroy all. They blast rocks and scatter them on the ground. The rock says, "Don't! You are hurting me." But the white people pay no attention. When the Indians use rocks, they take little round ones for their cooking. . . . How can the

spirit of the earth like the white man? . . . Everywhere the white man has touched it, it is sore.[12]

I wish I could stop here, on this poignant note, concluding that the magical consciousness of the shaman would be adequate for our post-modern world. But the matter is more complicated.

First, it is obvious from the quotation that the shaman's consciousness is perfectly congruent with the simple lifestyles, and above all the simple craft traditions, of the Indians. The magical consciousness restrained the crafts developed by the Indians; and in return the restrained, organic craft traditions supported the possibility of living with an I-thou attitude towards nature. This is very beautiful; but modern society is too complex, and there are too many people to expect that post-modern society will be able to live by shaking acorns from the trees and picking up small round stones for its fires. Short of catastrophic destruction (which, alas, is always a vivid possibility in any discussion of such matters) the post-modern world, as we noted in chapter 3, will be in need of elaborate technological life-support systems to feed and house great, though stabilizing, populations. *Different* technologies from characteristically modern ones, of course, will be the order of the day. Sophisticated solar energy collectors and means of storage, probably, in place of obsolescent oil refineries or hazardous nuclear plants—and the like. Recycling technologies. Miniaturization. But the point remains that the post-modern world will require *post*-modern technologies, not *pre*-modern ones. And the magical consciousness, unable to compromise with the scientific world view or method, seems a dubious candidate for running the machines and advancing the discoveries that a livable post-modern world will require to stay alive. If disaster strikes, of course, the occult consciousness may well be the mythic matrix of post-modernity; but if our hope here is to search for a form of consciousness adequate for a humane and livable future, the eyes of fire alone seem not enough.

A second danger comes in the echo of a question I left hanging in connection with the uncompromisable gap between astrology and the scientific world view; "Are there to be no limits to credulity in post-modern consciousness?" It is all very well to rejoice in the values of at-homeness in the universe, but what about the values of truth? It is beautiful to see purposes and meaning in all of nature, but what about integrity to evidence? Once such integrity is abandoned, must everything that is asserted be believed? What divides responsible belief from dangerous, deranged nonsense?

Here I confess again my respect for the austere virtues of genuine science. Resistance to authority, the discrimination between warranted and unwarranted assertions, the readiness to put treasured convictions (ideally, at any rate) on the scales of colleague confirmation—these are the great virtues of modernity *and are still virtues,* despite their inherent limitations when worshiped as supreme or sole.

What is the alternative to retaining them, somehow, in any post-modern consciousness that would deserve respect? Roszak dismisses objective consciousness as "an arbitrary construct in which a given society in a given historical situation has invested its sense of meaningfulness and value. And so," he concludes, "like any mythology, it can be gotten round and called into questions by cultural movements which find meaning and values elsewhere."[13] But I doubt that it is easy to "get around" the cultural values of objectivity without running the gravest risks.

These risks are not merely in personal integrity of belief, though this is important enough to give us second thoughts, but also in social terror. If post-modern consciousness has no defense against credulity, not only will we expect the grossest superstition to flourish in individual minds but also cruel public fanaticisms of all sorts: literal witch hunts again, voodoo torments, cruel tortures—such as even the admired Indians, we recall, were sometimes practitioners.

This brings me to my third warning. What is there in magical consciousness to act as a barrier against abuses of the

occult in familiar, exploitive ways? To see the "magic" in
nature with our eyes of fire may, as we have noted, call forth
moral reactions of restraint, which would be all to the good
both of nature and of man. But the history of magic also—
perhaps even more prominently—contains the history of
manipulation, greed, and exploitation "by other means" and
"through other laws" of compulsion. The black arts may not
be so far, in the mood and motive of their orgin, from the
sciences as the recent apologists of magic have suggested.
Historian of science Eugenio Garin sees them as very close,
"for magic is a practical activity which aims at the
transformation of nature by interfering with the laws of nature
through technical knowledge of how they operate."[14] If so,
the dreadful specter arises of a post-modern society combining
the worst aspects of exploitative modern consciousness with
the worst aspects of rampant credulity and superstition.

We may shudder at these thoughts. But our concern is not a
new one. The biblical religions, both Judaism and Christianity,
have traditionally warned against the seductive promises of
magic. They never denied the possibility or reality of the
occult, of course. The existence of witchcraft and divination is
assumed in both the Old and New Testaments, and the church
fathers wrote extensively about it. The biblical position on the
occult was fiercely hostile: "Thou shalt not suffer a witch to
live" was probably the rule even when Saul, disobeying his
own law, stole away to consult the necromancy of the witch
at Endor (1 Sam. 28). In the New Testament we find dramatic
conflicts between the early apostles and magicians with whom,
as miracleworkers, they were often confused. But the
Christians insisted that their power was solely the power of the
righteous God, operating "in the name of Jesus Christ;" while
the powers invoked by the rivals were unrighteous because
proudly independent of the sources of all being and goodness.

The ultimate control by goodness was the crucial point to
the apostles and to the church fathers as well. Tertullian, for
example, writes an interpretation of the three Wise Men—the

"Magi" of Eastern magic, the Babylonian astrologers who followed the stars to Bethlehem—in which their gifts at the manger symbolize their giving up of magic arts and turning over all such power to the incarnate God. To reinforce their reforms, as Tertullian tells the story, they "went home by another way."[15]

St. Augustine also discusses the occult, particularly astrology. For Augustine astrology was perfectly possible but *wrong.* Knowledge gained through the occult arts symbolizes forbidden knowledge, the outbreak of human pride. Power gained through magic symbolizes forbidden control, the clinging to other security than proper faith in God.

Such criticisms raise an interesting thought: what of Christianity itself as the matrix for the post-modern world? A change is on its way, like it or not, as we have seen. Christianity offers an actual alternative both to modern objective consciousness and to the occult. Christianity, indeed, has been engaged in battle with both over long centuries. Is Christianity merely a fossil, a denatured remnant of the pre-modern world? Or may there be enough life in this once-great form of consciousness to serve again as the matrix for another civilization? I shall next turn to Christianity's prospects of rising to this historic opportunity and to its possible place in the post-modern world.

Notes

1. Thomas S. Kuhn, *The Structure of Scientific Revolutions,* 2nd ed. (Chicago: University of Chicago Press, 1970), p. 77.
2. Carlos Castaneda, *A Separate Reality* (New York: Pocket Books, 1972). *See also* his *The Teachings of Don Juan: A Yaqui Way of Knowledge* (New York: Ballantine Books, 1968).
3. Sheila Ostrander and Lynn Schroeder, *Psychic Discoveries Behind the Iron Curtain* (Englewood Cliffs, N.J.: Prentice-Hall, 1970).
4. Peter Tompkins and Christopher Bird, *The Secret Life of Plants* (New York: Harper & Row, 1974).
5. J. B. Rhine, *Parapsychology: Frontier Science of the Mind* (Springfield, Ill.: C. C. Thomas, 1972). *See also* his *Progress in Parapsychology* (Durham, N.C.: Parapsychology Press, 1971).
6. Cited, with interesting conclusions drawn, in Kuhn, *The Structure of Scientific Revolutions,* p. 63.
7. Art Rosenblum and Leah Jackson, *The Natural Birth Control Book* (Philadelphia: Aquarian Research Foundation, 1974).
8. Eugenio Garin, *Science and Civic Life in the Italian Renaissance,* trans. Peter Munz (Garden City, N.Y.: Doubleday, 1969), p. 162.
9. Roszak, *The Making of a Counter Culture,* p. 244.
10. Ibid., p. 248.
11. Monod, *Chance and Necessity,* p. 169.
12. Quoted from Lee, *Freedom and Culture,* in Roszak, *The Making of a Counter Culture,* p. 245.
13. Roszak, *The Making of a Counter Culture,* p. 215.
14. Garin, *Science and Civic Life,* p. 146.
15. Tertullian, *De Idolatria;* cited in Dijksterhuis, *The Mechanization of the World Picture,* p. 95.

5. GOD OF NATURE

Christianity has long waged its battle on two fronts important to our transitionary world: against scientistic reductionism and against occult apostasy. Christianity is still a social force to be reckoned with, despite its long series of losses to modern consciousness and its nearly complete absorption into an "official" culture form. Might it be possible for Christianity to bridge our current transition and take on new life as the adequate religious matrix for the post-modern world?

In many ways this is an intriguing suggestion. Christianity has already proved its power not only to survive vast historical upheavals but also to create a civilization after the transition. The change from rural Palestine to imperial Rome shows Christianity's resilience under altered conditions; the change from fallen Rome to medieval Paris shows Christianity's power to mold new forms. Even the fact that Christianity as a religion has been able to survive the fall of its own distinctive civilization and continue as well as it has through the three centuries of the modern world is impressive. I am reminded of

Arnold Toynbee's hypothesis, likening the rising and falling of successive civilizations to the chariot wheels of history, on which the great religions of mankind advance. Perhaps the fall of the modern and the rise of the post-modern world should be welcomed by Christians as yet another opportunity for renewed life. What does the Christian world-picture offer that might be helpful for post-modern consciousness?

A primary point to note is that the Christian world-picture is not in the first place a theory or a set of doctrines but, rather, a set of stories and images evocative of attitudes and provocative of theological interpretation. These interpretations have differed—sometimes widely—over the ages, and (as we shall see later in this chapter) may quite possibly differ still more as historical circumstances change. Still, one great interpretive framework has dominated most of the history of Christian thought and feeling in the West: it is the framework of "being" derived from Greek philosophy through which the stories and images of the Christian world-picture have traditionally been seen. Especially since the thirteenth-century synthesis of biblical *mythos* with Aristotelian *logos* achieved by St. Thomas Aquinas, there has been a Christian consciousness that deserves recognition as "mainstream." Other "streams" have existed and may yet come into prominence, but mainstream Christianity needs our notice first.

The principal feature of the mainstream Christian worldview, fashioned from biblical images perceived through Aristotelian categories, is that nature was created from nothing by the sovereign God, Lord of all being. Traditional Christian consciousness cannot overstress the sense that absolutely all ultimate power resides in God. He is dependent on nothing for his being or his actions. The world is dependent for everything on God. All the seeming powers of the world are in reality "delegated," as it were, from the Holy Center of all powers; all the world's reality is creaturely reality, contingent upon God's creative will and sustaining action. God's absoluteness is so great, some medieval doctrine held, that he cannot be considered relative in any way, not even to the degree of being related to the world. The world is related to God, of course, but the logic of this relation is not reciprocal; God is not related to the world, though the world is related to him. Another medieval doctrine drew the consequences that God could not be supposed to know the world directly, since cognition is a kind of relation. But God cannot be thought ignorant of the world, either! Instead God knows the world (perfectly) through his perfect knowledge of himself as its source of being, but the creative power does not establish a relation or make God "relative" in any way.

I repeat these doctrines not merely to titillate with crumbs of medieval logic but rather to underscore the lengths to which traditional Christian thought once went to defend the fundamental value of God's absoluteness. This absoluteness is not in power alone. All ultimate worth, as well, resides in God. God's goodness is complete. The world adds nothing essential. The world minus God equals zero; God minus the world equals perfection. Indeed, the world's worth, such as it has, is entirely derived from God's calling it good. Like the world's reality, its worth is genuine so long as God wills it, but it is derivative worth. Creaturely worth is nothing in itself or apart from God. "Neo-orthodox" Protestant theologians like Karl Barth in this century have underlined this point by insisting that creatures may claim no independent value apart from God lest they "boast themselves against God."[1] Even God's love for the world, as Anders Nygren argued, is entirely unmotivated by being attracted to any value the world could boast. Such attracted love is *eros:* needy, hungering for values it does not have. But God hungers after nothing. His love is always *agape:* full, unselfseeking, impossible for fallen men to emulate but only to receive in faith.[2]

The other side of this mainstream worldview, however, is that the domain of nature has been entrusted to mankind by God's decree. The human race is also creature, of course, and therefore has merely creaturely (derivative) reality and worth.

But humanity, uniquely among creatures, was made "in the image of God" and thus (however the "image" is interpreted) has a special status in the world. While still definitely under God's ultimate authority, mankind has been put in charge of the rest of the world of creatures. Adam is told to subdue the earth, and fill it. Man symbolizes his superiority by giving names to the lower orders. The world belongs to us by right, to use as needed. But we are finally responsible to God for our stewardship.

How does this great viewpoint commend itself to the needs of post-modern mankind? On the same criteria we have been applying to other fundamental spiritual outlooks, what shall we say of mainstream Christianity?

There are very significant virtues. Man's tendency to self-assertion is put under ultimate authority. The anthropocentric hubris of the modern world is limited by other values. These values center in God, finally; but nature, too, may benefit from Christian consciousness if God is pictured as valuing "even the least of these." Let me illustrate. It is sometimes almost pathetic to listen to well-meaning environmentalists try to justify, in narrowly anthropocentric modern-consciousness terms, why some endangered species should be protected even at some cost or inconvenience to human life. How can the western sheepherder be convinced that the endangered eagles that cost him a portion of his profit should be legally defended against his pursuit? Will life be that much poorer for future generations who have never seen them if Africa loses her leopards or Florida her alligators? The strained and roundabout arguments of anthropocentric modern consciousness are seldom very convincing—when the chips are really down. If the only appeal allowed by the fundamental religious frame of reference is to some *human* interest or long-term benefit or aesthetic need, then alas for the vanishing wetlands, the birds of prey, and the bearers of exotic furs or hides! To say that any diminution in nature diminishes each one of us is attractive sloganeering, but how many can honestly say they personally feel the pinch? There are few, I fear; too few to carry the day. And even for those who believe that such arguments to long-term human interests are valid and convincing,[3] all other things being equal, how many would weigh such indirect diminution of interests more heavily than some clear, immediate, "hardheaded" cost on the other side?

The Christian consciousness can answer these questions less awkwardly, more directly, than the purely anthropocentric modern ethic will allow. The Christian can reply simply that golden eagles should be valued because God created them a species and still cares about them. In a community of creatures, under God, no single set of values (all human) is entitled to carry the day. God's mysterious way in forming even "Leviathan" must be respected by the man of faith (Job 38–42).

In the same way, the sheer fact that man is pictured as under moral restraints grounded beyond his own will or purposes may help post-modern society to accept needed social and economic restraints that must come, willy-nilly, before long. One of the most pressing issues facing modern mankind is the manner in which human pride and greed can be effectively prevented from continuing the mad press toward growth in all sectors—population, consumption, investment, pollution, depletion—that must lead to terrible rending of the modern world's social fabric. If Christianity, which once nurtured the relatively stable feudal society, can now sustain the steady-state post-modern world, it will have gone far toward offering worldly, as well as heavenly, salvation.

In addition to these virtues, the Christian vision would offer post-modern man a richer content of experience than modern man has enjoyed. Return to Christianity would reestablish the meaningful covenant, between humanity and the larger universe, that was broken by the rise of the objective consciousness. The world could be seen and felt again as home for qualities and meanings long since driven out by the austere vision of traditional scientism. And all this could be gained, in contrast to the occult consciousness, with greater moral guidance than the sense of magic alone can provide. The self-limiting or self-critical element we found missing in occultism is present in traditional Christianity's humbling vision of the all-righteous creator God.

All this is well worth praising, but mainstream Christianity leaves several vital points to be desired, despite these great strengths. I shall recount three weaknesses in mainstream Christianity and then ask whether they are essential to Christianity itself or whether, somehow, a non-Aristotelian, post-modern Christianity, better than mainstream Christianity at just these points—but still Christianity—can be conceived.

First, I find it a significant weakness in mainstream Christianity that all values in nature are merely extrinsic and derivative. Mankind stands accountable, true, but only to God, not to the vulnerable earth. God's absolute monopoly of first-order being and worth leaves the world around us with only surrogate status. This status alone, if protected by a keen awareness of God's stern interest in all his creatures—his "keeping them covered," as it were, by his concern—*might*, as I have said, afford protection to nature and enforce restraint on mankind against excesses of exploitation and abuse. I regret, however, to point out that such restraint has not been a noteworthy effect of mainstream Christianity in the past. True, some important traditions within Christianity have dealt tenderly with nature: gentle Saint Francis looked on all creatures as his siblings and Saint Benedict founded an order that would treat farmwork as a form of prayerful service. But in the mainstream of Christianity, as the historian Lynn White and others have effectively argued,[4] the Genesis commandment from God himself to man that man "multiply and subdue the earth" has had the opposite effect altogether: it has tended to sanctify limitless exploitation and uncontrolled population growth. God's command seems to whip man on in his desire to possess and control and use. Far from "keeping them covered," God seems in the biblical image to be sanctifying, with his ultimate moral authority, the ravaging of his nonhuman creatures. W. Lee Humphreys, scholar of biblical Hebrew, reinforces this point by noting that the Hebrew word *kābash,* translated "subdue" in the Genesis story, is also associated with contexts, like "trampling down" the grapes in a winepress, like "vanquishing" one's enemies, like using a "footstool," that suggest a harsh line against nature. There is even an overtone of rape in the word, since it is the term used when the wicked Haman was thought by the returning King Ahasuerus to have "forced" Queen Esther (Esther 7:8).[5] I doubt therefore that mainstream Christian consciousness, leaving nature entirely dependent on God's concern for its protection against man's abuse, is adequate for the needs of the post-modern world. God, in instructing man to "subdue" and utilize, seems not concerned enough, in this picture, with the need for human restraint. In the days of ancient Hebrew life, of course, the need for such restraint was not so visible as it is today. The world was hardly at all exploited, and human beings were few. But the God who instructs man to "vanquish," "trample down," "force" nature is not the God whose advice a desirable consciousness could take uncritically. Likewise the God who urges populations to multiply can hardly be worshiped by a society grown familiar with the fatal consequences of exponential curves.

Second, I wonder whether the value implications of the mainstream Christian interpretation of God will be able to draw instinctive favorable response in post-modern men and women. The traditional view reflects the ancient oriental attitude toward absolute potentates—carried to infinity. The king can do no wrong, his will alone is sovereign and before it even the mighty, who serve solely at his pleasure, tremble and abase themselves. The very essence of the state resides in him. His slightest wish is instantly obeyed, and those who displease him are subjected to prolonged and hopeless torture. So likewise is God to the world, in the traditional picture—his absoluteness even requires a new logic of relations. But can, or should, post-modern men and women "go home again" to such values? The modern world has experienced much since the days of the Pharaohs. There are still absolute masters, of course, but centuries of moral investment have gone into widespread intuitions that there may be another, better way in which personal dignity may be preserved even in relationship with legitimate ruling power, and in which rulers interact with and are limited by the intrinsic rights and interests of the governed. Should we expect post-modern men and women to abandon these hard-won intuitions? If adequate post-modern, not pre-modern, forms of consciousness are what we are in search of, the world-pictures involved must focus and reinforce at least the best of modern sensibilities. In this the mainstream Christian interpretation of God is seriously defective.

Third, and finally, I must in philosophical conscience return once more to the problem of credulity. The question is not only whether mainstream Christianity can sustain an ecologically sound society, not only whether Christianity so interpreted can support fundamental moral intuitions, but also —and not least—whether traditional Christianity can be *believed* without opening the floodgates fatally wide. In asking this question I am not assuming that modern science is the final authority on what is responsibly believable. But we saw in the last chapter that warranted belief on some kind of standard is needed to sort out the wheat from the cognitive chaff. Mainstream Christianity has not traditionally been enthusiastic about the offering of warrants for independent judgment, thus subjecting its value-laden assertions to tests of responsible belief. Even philosophically acute thinkers like Saint Thomas Aquinas acknowledged the fundamental role of authority. Within the boundaries of authority energetic argumentation could and did take place, but always within the "theological circle." Ought post-modern consciousness to be expected to "turn itself in" to arbitrary authority (any authority is arbitrary which refuses to stand accountable for its claims by offering reasons, not anathemas, to its challengers) after feeling the genuine force of duty represented by modern responsibility of belief? I think not. In this respect traditional Christianity fails to cohere with the best in modern methods of thought.

Thus I conclude that the mainstream version of the Christian world-picture is a dubious link to post-modernity. Whatever an adequate post-modern religious matrix will be like, it needs to be in touch with the best of modern values and of modern thinking if it is to bridge the gap constructively from this historical epoch to the next. This was once strikingly true of Christianity as it served as link from Roman to medieval civilizations. Christianity managed to incorporate most of the highest of the classical values, and was fortunate in having, in its ranks, intellectuals like St. Augustine capable of using the best of classical philosophy as vehicle for interpreting Christian imagery for the faithful and for the critic alike. Today our best values have undergone some change; our best cognitive vehicles have been further refined since Plato and Aristotle. Might it be that Christianity could rise to the historical challenge once again and develop a *nontraditional but still Christian* version qualified to carry the new day as once it carried the old?

II

I think we should be cautious in answering any such grandly speculative question, but I am not inclined to dismiss the possibility. Contemporary theologians are at work on a number of fronts. One of these, for example, is the effort to articulate the Christian matrix of value-laden image and story in the terms or in a manner drawn from the philosophical approach of Ludwig Wittgenstein. Another active front is the campaign to "demythologize" Christian imagery and interpret it in a way undergirded by the existential philosophy of Martin Heidegger. A third area of theological activity is attempting to understand the biblical *mythos* along the lines of Alfred North

Whitehead's philosophy of organism, or "process philosophy," as it is usually called. There are other movements as well, "political theologies," "liberation theologies," "theologies of hope," theologies based on theories of Marx, or of Hegel, or of Comte, or of avant garde psychology.

In all these cases the adopted or constructed theory acts as an interpretive conceptual framework (much as did the philosophy of Plato for St. Augustine or the philosophy of Aristotle for St. Thomas Aquinas)—this conceptual framework facilitating, clarifying, organizing serious attempts to think in terms of the great, definitive value-focusing imagery of the Christian tradition. The imagery, as I maintained in chapter 1, is primary for religious consciousness. But as I also noted, in passing, the theory is important too. The theological theory not only expresses the value-imagery, as best its categories allow, but also it inevitably influences, by its way of organizing and categorizing, what the imagery is felt as signifying. That is, to put it another way, we turn to various theoretical frameworks (often philosophies) to help us think connectedly, in keeping with our primary religious images, which these theories are supposed to articulate, interpret, clarify, and relate to the rest of our beliefs. But as we become used to thinking our religious images in terms of one framework or another, the imagery itself is perceived differently. One framework will draw a certain aspect of the richly varied imagery to the foreground, casting other aspects into the shadowy background as "merely figurative;" another will select different aspects as central to primary meaning.

If we assume that the fundamental imagery of Christianity is what defines it for worship, not the theoretical frameworks that variously serve to articulate that imagery for thought, then Christianity may remain truly Christian in the essential religious sense while being very much transformed at the level of theory. We have seen this happen, at least once, when Saint Thomas scandalized the theological world in his day by adopting the philosophy of Aristotle for his vehicle in interpreting Christian faith. Hitherto Christianity had been set in a Platonic framework. Aristotle, Plato's pupil and severe critic, was perceived, when rediscovered, as an enemy of Christianity. But St. Thomas showed that Aristotle was only the enemy of certain Platonic theoretical elements, not of Christian faith itself, which could be acceptably articulated in the new Aristotelian framework. His efforts were so successful in the thirteenth century that we tend to forget today how radical they then seemed to his contemporaries.

But today even deeper changes in theory are afoot. Both Plato and Aristotle agreed on certain theoretical fundamentals that were characteristic of classical Greek thinking but that are being challenged today. Both agreed, for a prime example, that being—true being—could not be changeable in any way. They agreed that being was more perfect than becoming, or than anything subject to change. They both had a place in their philosophies for a highest being, one which could not change in any way or even know change. For Plato this highest being was entirely impersonal, the Form of the Good; for Aristotle this being was eternally aloof Thought thinking only Itself.

These Greek philosophical convictions were of course imported into Christian theology when Christian intellectuals adopted the best theoretical framework available for the articulation of their faith. On the whole it seems entirely natural—even inevitable—after centuries of thinking in these terms. But there were costs incurred by so doing. The dynamic creator-sustainer of the biblical imagery had somehow to be thought in terms of classical Greek repugnance to change of any sort. As highest being, God could not any longer be thought to be making decisions, engaging in work (no matter how effortless), or interacting with the events of rebellious human history. As absolute, in the framework of Plato and Aristotle, God could not be thought (as distinct from felt) as related by concern for, knowledge of, or providential intention toward the world of finitude and becoming. Above all, he could never be thought on this framework to be frustrated, as he seems to be over and over again in the primary religious imagery, or as momentarily angry, or as changing his mind ("repenting himself")[6] about everything. All the stories in which God is so pictured must move into the background, on this theoretical reading, as merely figurative expressions. Other passages stressing the otherness of God from changing worldly things—especially the mysterious announcement from the burning bush, "I AM WHO I AM" (Exod. 3:14), suggesting that God is Being Itself—move forward into prominence as expressing basic truth.

It all seems quite natural, and as we have seen at the start of this chapter it is basic to mainstream Christianity's way of thinking its essential value imagery. But what if the ancient Greek theoretical premise about the primacy of *being* is challenged by a contemporary philosophy that is impressed by the fundamental place of dynamic *becoming* in this universe made out of constant, pulsing energy? Matter, we have learned, is nothing but events of energy. And energy is "becoming" in identifiable form, or process. Given such a theoretical base, what would Christianity look like? It would have an untraditional appearance, certainly; but if the essential religious imagery of God and Christ and man and nature could be rethought without forcing, might not a Christian faith qualified for the post-modern world then arise?

I shall conclude this chapter with a minisketch and assessment of this possibility. I do this mainly as an example of what hope there may be for flexible Christian responses to our historic needs in this transition time, but also partly because, of all the current theological reforms, this particular one, process theology, commends itself to me most strongly.

First, what are the general outlines of process theology? Its basic theoretical framework is drawn from the philosophy developed in this century by Alfred North Whitehead, a mathematician deeply interested in the startling developments of mathematical physics in our time. He begins with the un-Greek premise I suggested: that reality is inseparable from process, flux taking on form only to be transcended by more such events of process in the endless rhythm of this dynamic universe.

I must not even begin to develop his viewpoint or his arguments here, which are fascinating but technical and expressed in a vocabulary all his own.[7] I shall just say, very simply, that in Whitehead's framework there is a significant place for God, who is required for theoretical reasons in the system. God is the everlasting entity needed in this system as the actual font of all pure possibilities, the cosmic framer of general real possibilities, the intimate lure in the universe toward heightened value, and the final repository of all worthy achievement. His experience is of the world as its flux achieves and reachieves definition in the ceaseless dialectic of becoming. His love for the world is expressed in his unending effort to enhance the quality of achieved definiteness, hence the intrinsic value, of every self-creating entity at every moment and in every place. He is directly felt by men and women in both of his two major aspects: as the Abiding One ("Abide with me, fast falls the eventide" was one of Whitehead's favorite hymn citations), and as the Eros of the Universe, restlessly urging toward higher value.

More could be said, but it should already be clear that such a conceptual framework as Whitehead's must be interesting as making possible a fresh theoretical articulation of Christian imagery.[8] Any such articulation will necessarily conflict with the traditional one at crucial points, since the basic premise about being has been challenged; but this is to be expected when basic theoretical frameworks clash. This clash, however, should not be confused with an incompatibility between Whiteheadian philosophy and Christianity itself, unless the Whiteheadian framework is shown unable to articulate satisfactorily the primary value-imagery of biblical faith. May it prove adequate, despite its initial unfamiliarity?

God, first, on the Whiteheadian scheme, cannot be thought

to be unchanging in all respects. In one respect, in his aspect as primordial font of all pure possibility, he is unchanging; but in respect to his relationships to the world he is, like the rest of the universe, in process. He is even a growing God, moving everlastingly from perfection to greater perfection. This is literally unthinkable from an Aristotlian framework, of course, but there is much biblical imagery that can be seen as supporting such a dynamic deity, intimately relating to events as they develop and responding creatively to them. Indeed, it seems to me, this is the far more natural way of reading most of the stories of the Bible involving God. These images are dynamic—the voice from the whirlwind awing Job; the guide and military guardian of the Israelites leading out of Egypt and into the Promised Land; the urging, prodding, threatening, punishing, forgiving God who sends his Son at the fullness of time and receives him back after his atoning sacrifice. Surely such images are more naturally articulated by process theology than by the utterly static categories of Greek thought? Here, where there is a conflict, process theology would seem clearly superior to traditional Christian forms of thought.

God, second, cannot on Whiteheadian grounds be thought to be absolute creator of the world and eternally independent of it. Instead he is to be conceived as an orderer and lure toward more valuable sorts of achieved order; he is coeverlasting with the world, and as much dependent on the world as the world is dependent on him. Again this is shocking to many ingrained habits of thought, but a look at the Genesis imagery itself will show that the theological doctrine of *creatio ex nihilo* is not obviously there—it has had to be read into the understanding of the story by generations of traditional interpretation. What the story itself shows, it may be argued, is an ordering God "starting out" with a disordered or chaotic world already before him: "And the earth was waste and void; and darkness was upon the face of the deep; and the Spirit of God moved upon the face of the waters" (Gen. 1:2). Again the Whiteheadian articulation seems at least as appropriate to the imagery of faith as its distinguished traditional predecessors.

There are other differences. The world, on process theology's interpretation, would have genuine value of its own as well as being of its own. This might give a renewed force to the phrase: "and God saw that it was good" (Gen. 1:10). Finite goodness, that is, would no longer be a matter merely of God's arbitrary fiat but would be due to something intrinsic in things themselves. And if this is so, then man and God, though far from equal, are in a distinct way cocreators of value. Man has dignity, freedom, and rights of his own. God is man's legitimate leader and guide into the good, and into the better; God is never a sheer despot.

So much, then, for this minisketch of the outlines of process theology. Its virtues, measured against the needs of the post-modern world, are evident at once. On the practical side, it would provide post-modern consciousness a sense of organismic unity with nature and of the presence of intrinsic values in the world; it would offer a time-tested matrix of Christian imagery that could provide a sense of the meaningful place of human effort in a significant universe; it would reinforce ecological values and guide post-modern consciousness into the saving ways of restraint and wise holistic policies; and it would reflect the best of modern intuitions about human dignity, freedom, and the proper reciprocity between government and governed.

Its cognitive or intellectual virtues are similarly strong. It is carefully reasoned, showing respect for the legitimate modern sense of obligation to integrity of thought but without the devaluing, antiseptic abstractions that have flawed consciousness. And it is coherent with—no, rooted in—the major scientific results of the twentieth century: quantum mechanics, relativity theory, matter-energy convertibility, and the like. More than at the vital edge of science alone, it is coherent also with important developments in educational theory, with the widening appreciation of world religions, and with respected theories of art, history, and society. Christian process theology offers impressively strong credentials, therefore, both practically and intellectually, as candidate for the adequate religious matrix needed by the post-modern world. It would present a post-modern version of Christianity that might actually satisfy our most urgent requirements.

So I end this chapter . . . almost. The happy ending is not quite so simply written as this discussion of process theology might suggest. There are still problems to be met and strategies for their solution to be suggested. One obvious problem is: Can process theology be *accepted* as Christian by Christians? If we are looking for religious answers to profound historical needs, a scholar's philosophy alone can hardly satisfy. Only if process philosophy becomes effective process theology—or, better still, simply mainstream post-modern Christianity, as the great images are freshly understood—can large changes in social policy and common consciousness be hoped for. Philosophy, though it plays a vital role in the total economy of things, is an elite craft. We need power and mass appeal in addition to adequacy, in principle, for life and thought. The verdict on process theology, however, is still pending. It will be given in this larger sense not by philosophers like myself but by clergymen as they preach and laymen as they respond to the new ways of articulating the old, old story. The verdict will come, in other words, from the believing community whose judgment on the appropriateness of the new way of thinking to the articulation of the images they revere will be—and of right should be—final.[9] What shall we do *in the meanwhile,* while the fateful process goes on?

Another problem yet to be faced is: can process theology, or any other metaphysical position, be wholeheartedly *believed* under today's disconcerting transitional conditions? However well recommended as socially needed or as abstractly well credentialed, this question remains for any comprehensive religious view of the world. Perhaps the times simply are not ripe for such neat, inclusive views. I suspect, for many of us, this may be the hardest problem of all.

Notes

1. Karl Barth, *Church Dogmatics: A Selection* (New York: Harper & Row, 1969), *passim*.

2. Anders Nygren, *Agape and Eros* (New York: Harper & Row, 1969).

3. *See,* for a strong example of such an argument, George Vetz and Donald Lee Johnson, "Breaking the Web," *Environment* 16, no. 10 (December 1974), pp. 31–39.

4. Lynn White, Jr., "The Historical Roots of Our Ecologic Crisis," *Science* 155 (10 March 1967).

5. W. Lee Humphreys, "Pitfalls and Promises of Biblical Texts as a Basis for a Theology of Nature," in *A New Ethic for a New Earth,* ed. Glenn C. Stone for the Faith-Man-Nature Group (New York: Friendship Press, 1971), pp. 99 ff.

6. *See,* for example, the motive attributed to God for sending the Flood (Gen. 6:6).

7. Whitehead's primary statement was in *Process and Reality: An Essay in Cosmology* (New York: The Humanities Press, 1929). A useful aid in reading it is Donald W. Sherburne's *A Key to Whitehead's Process and Reality* (New York: Macmillan, 1966).

8. An important effort in this direction was made by John B. Cobb, Jr., in *A Christian Natural Theology: Based on the Thought of Alfred North Whitehead* (Philadelphia: The Westminster Press, 1965).

9. For amplification of this point, *see* my *Basic Modern Philosophy of Religion,* pp. 380–386.

6. SENSE OF MYSTERY

We are on a quest, in this book, for a vital and adequate religious response to the current transition from the modern to the post-modern world. We saw in part 1 the pressing need to go beyond the technolatrous objective *mythos* of modern consciousness that has served the modern world so well—and so badly—as its functioning religious matrix. In part 2 we have noted the possible return of magical consciousness as an alternative deserving much respect but even more caution. And most recently we have considered Christianity as a viable candidate for shaping post-modern consciousness—not traditional mainstream Christianity, which we saw to suffer serious weaknesses, but a post-modern rearticulation of the great archetypal images of biblical faith through an organismic, ecologically holistic, scientifically relevant process theology. The benefits of such a dynamic, post-modern version of Christianity, we saw, would be (1) a new-sensed unity with the natural environment, (2) a new realization of responsibility toward nature involving needed restraints on human exploitation, (3) a new appreciation of the virtues of scientific standards of warranted belief without the characteristic modern defects of alienative reductionism, and (4) a new lease on effective life for the ancient and powerful value-expressive and value-focusing imagery of the biblical heritage.

Before rejoicing in the successful conclusion of our quest, however, I raised two cautions that seem to me serious and in need of thoughtful attention. One of these cautions had to do with the question whether process theology will ever be accepted by Christians as the appropriate articulation of their faith. Lacking such sensed religious appropriateness and left to itself as a technical system of concepts, Whiteheadian philosophy of organism is most unlikely to be a major force in shaping post-modern consciousness; but the verdict is still out and is likely to remain so for some time. What should be our strategy in the meantime—a period which may well last longer than our lives?

The second caution had to do with the even more general question whether these times of turmoil and transition are suitable for any great religious synthesis. Even if process theology is quickly deemed *appropriate* by the Christian religious community, can we assume widespread *conviction* to follow, given the current situation? Assuming adequate metaphysical credentials, if they can be agreed upon, and assuming religious appropriateness, can we—Christians or non-Christians—believe it (or any such) fully enough to expect that our lives will be changed, our consciousness altered, and our society saved? This, after all, is not a wholly voluntary matter. If there are serious grounds to doubt the probable effectiveness of any great religious metaphysical synthesis during the unstable transition time we face before us, then we had better develop a strategy for dealing realistically and constructively with our actual situation. Post-modern Christianity may be well suited for a desirable post-modern world, but such a world does not exist. What does exist? How should we cope, not *sometime,* but *now?*

I

I submit that we are currently in a poor intellectual and valuational situation for the nourishment of great religious-metaphysical synthesis, and thus for the time being we shall have to develop other strategies of survival not dependent upon thinking that we see very clearly or very whole.

Consider, first, our current intellectual situation. The sheer fact is that our best knowledge is so shot through with mystery that to call it knowledge may some day seem a little arrogant and quaint. I was given a pungent taste of this fact recently when, on the occasion of the five-hundredth anniversary of Copernicus's birth I was invited to participate in a conference, sponsored in Washington jointly by the Smithsonian Institution and the National Academy of Science, to celebrate both the memory of Copernicus and the advances of current cosmology. The outcome from the latter point of view was fascinating and more than a little funny. Distinguished scientist after distinguished scientist rose to present papers on how much easier it was to (seem to) understand the universe in the days of Copernicus! They were not saying this in so many words, for the most part, but in total effect their presentations reinforced vividly how strange and deeply mysterious the known—or the thought-to-be-known—universe of current astronomy and cosmic physics must be recognized to be. It occurred to me that I was there hearing the authentic voice of post-modern science—of science no longer easily categorizable as "modern" in the familiar style of the last three hundred years. There was little of the attitude of controlling hubris, of reductive materialism, of confident progressivism at that historic conference. Instead I heard of mysterious entities, hidden energy sources, baffling results that force leading astronomers to wonder aloud whether their whole picture of things may be wrong in fundamental ways. Even our closest neighbor, the moon, is more of a mystery than ever. Our space explorations have given us vast new amounts of data and have ruled out certain theories of the solar system, but in some ways our puzzlement is even greater that it was before. Much more, then, the mysteries opened up by the discovery of "black holes" in space, the contents of which must forever remain unknown since no signal or information of any kind could in principle get out to us. Or the discovery of quasars, generating energy at theoretically impossible levels. Or bafflingly powerful X-ray emitters. Or inexplicably regular radio sources. So on and on. What seems most characteristic of post-modern astronomy—like all post-modern science—is put well by William Pollard when he says:

> It should be evident from all this that when we speak of "mystery" in science we no longer mean unknown areas or puzzles which research in the future may be expected to clear up. We are not speaking of a mystery of anything unknown at all. Rather we are speaking of the mysteriously amazing character of the known. There is a true mystery of the known and our modern knowledge in science confronts us with that mystery very strongly.[1]

Certainly this intellectual situation is much more pervasive than astronomy or cosmology alone. Closer to home on earth, as intimately as within the atoms of our own bodies, the mysteries deepen in the elusive world of submicroscopic physics. The tendency of modern science, as we saw in earlier chapters, has been to analyze matter into its smallest particles, seeking the fundamental reality in the smallest fragment. Smaller and yet smaller particles have resulted from this determined drive downward, each "elementary" particle giving way to still more "elementary" ones as more and more accelerators are built to develop energies strong enough to smash the atom into still tinier bits. Nature seems all too cooperative! Each larger hammer splatters the atom still further, so far without limit, in principle, and without evoking any coherent theory. "Fundamental particle physics is a mess," one expert friend complained to me succinctly. There are too many particles, now; there is no rhyme or reason to them all; the feeling is of Chinese boxes opening to show smaller boxes inside without limit.

Another friend, physicist Harold Schilling whose consciousness of his field is emphatically post-modern, suggested in conversation that the problem may be in the basic assumptions of modern physics, not in nature. Just before the Copernican revolution, he reminded me, the techniques of astronomy were refined to the point that each careful new observation required the postulation of a new epicycle to be added to account for the phenomena. To the pre-Copernicans each must have seemed like an important discovery, however frustratingly complex nature seemed to be. Perhaps, urged Schilling, we are asking an analogously wrong question of the atom by trying to split it into its supposedly fundamental particles. Perhaps "elementary particles" are theoretical fictions analogous to the epicycles of the pre-Copernicans. Perhaps we need a revolutionary new way of conceiving the atom not as built up out of tiny particles but as capable of manifesting particlelike behavior under certain conditions.

Later, at the recently mentioned Copernicus Conference, I broached this question in conversation with the distinguished physicist Werner Heisenberg, father of the immensely significant "uncertainty principle" of fundamental physics. Heisenberg agreed immediately that the quest for particles was leading nowhere and was deeply misguided. I asked him whether he had some guess about what theoretical approach to the atom might point the way to needed revolutions in physics. His answer: consider the atom in terms of "mathematical resonances," not tiny bits of anything.

William Pollard, another post-modern physicist and valued friend, prefers to think of the atom as made up of *quarks,* tripartite entities which can never exist except in combination —"one in three and three in one." Whether Trinitarian quarks or Pythagorean resonances, or something else, the atom is a source of mystery today. Matter itself is far from understood;

far less, then, is it capable of being the paradigm of explanation by which everything else can be understood. Pollard writes:

> The old materialism which reduced everything to simple masses in motion has been swept away. The contemporary materialist must visualize material reality in terms of matter and anti-matter waves in a kind of shadow world, and consider them to be made up of mass, charge, nuclearity, and other basic constituents according to various recipes. It is a strange and shadowy kind of materialism with none of the simple, substantial, and sturdy obviousness of the old established kind.[2]

In this context the recent triumph of molecular biology in discovering the basic code through which all life transmits genetic information becomes the occasion both of admiration and of wonder. The coded "tape" made up of sugars and phosphoric acid, called nucleic acid, is wound in two strands in the famous double helix form. The complementary strands of nucleic acid contain all the information required for producing the whole organism it encodes. The chemical "letters" comprising the code spell out "words" directing the manufacture of various proteins. The words together make up genetic "sentences" and "paragraphs" leading to the masterpieces of living organisms in all their complexity and variety. In this discovery there is the basis for the keenest admiration.

There is also stimulus for wonder at even deeper mysteries. Gunther Stent, a molecular biologist, points out that the code is the same across all the vast gaps that differentiate life-forms —from bacteria to plants and to animals including mammals. The same few letters, that is, spell out the unimaginable richness of all living things. This is wonderful in itself, but it is even more amazing that the code has remained so stable through all the evolutionary time—billions of years—that such universality requires. Stent speculates about this amazing stability but offers no final answers. He goes on, then, to raise an even more baffling subject: "the general properties of the genetic code turn out to bear a curious resemblance," he writes, "to another symbolic system devised more than 3000 years ago for fathoming the nature of life, namely to the ancient *I Ching,* or 'Book of Changes' . . ."[3] Stent proceeds to describe the hexagrams of the *I Ching,* notes their astonishing anticipation of binary mathematics, and then concludes:

> But however surprising may be the anticipation of binary digits by the *I Ching,* the congruence between it and the genetic code is nothing short of amazing. For if Yang (the male, or light, principle) is identified with the purine bases and Yin (the female, or dark, principle) with pyrimidine bases, so that Old Yang and Yin correspond to the complementary adenine (A) and thymine (T) pair and New Yang and Yin to the complementary guanine (G) and cytosine (C) pair, each of the 64 hexagrams comes to represent one of the nucleotide triplet codons. The "natural" order of the *I Ching* can now be seen to generate an array of nucleotide triplets in which many of the generic codon relations manifest in Crick's arrangement are shown. Perhaps students of the presently still mysterious origins of the genetic code might consult the extensive commentaries of the *I Ching* to obtain some clues to the solution of their problem.[4]

This may merely be a curiosity, and Stent's final remark may be ironic, but it shows how far from simple reductive arrogance even triumphant molecular biology has come. And still more mysteries abound. Not only do the origin and amazing stability of the genetic code evade our understanding but also an unreducible "plus" stands out. That plus is information and meaning. William Pollard has said that one can no more reduce life to molecules than one can reduce Shakespeare's *Hamlet* to the paper and ink and type of the book in which it is printed.[5] A similar point was made by Barry Commoner a few years ago in a debate printed in the *Saturday Review.* Noting that DNA and RNA molecules never appear spontaneously in nature apart from living organisms, Commoner concluded that DNA is not the secret of life, but, on the contrary, that "life is the secret of DNA!"[6] We have learned much about the ways and means of genetic structure, but the mysteries of biology have not been eliminated; they have been driven deeper.

As we probe those depths our knowledge increases and so does our awareness of how much we do not understand. This is the key to all post-modern science. Harold Schilling sums it up well:

> It is important to recognize that it is all of science we are talking about, not just physics. Today's literature about science abounds in references not only to the new physics but to the new chemistry, new biology, new psychology, new anthropology, and still others, implying that a new day has dawned for science in general.[7]

All this has been in illustration of our current intellectual situation. The mysteries of post-modern science are so pervasive that it seems an inappropriate historical moment to pin our hopes on a great cognitive synthesis. A metaphysical scheme, to be adequate, must relate to the best knowledge of the time. But what firm ground is to be found today? There is excitement and hope as well as bafflement in the air; I do not mean to paint a bleak picture, just a realistic one in which surprises are more likely than closure for the foreseeable future.

On the other hand, and analogously, I think that our current valuational situation is unpropitious for the emergence of a great religious consensus based on any single *mythos*. We find ourselves in a time of radical pluralism regarding the images by which men and women picture their world and their preferences within it. The value-drenched images of technolatry are still viable for many, perhaps most, in our modern world; but, as we have seen, the power of such a *mythos* is bound to wane as objective consciousness and the modern world itself encounter historical nemesis. There are signs already, as I noted in chapter 4, that wholly different mythic forms are ready to challenge the unquestioned hegemony of those rooted in modern science.

The challenges are themselves startlingly varied. Simply by juxtaposing chapters on magic and Christianity—themselves ancient rivals—I have tried to suggest something of this variety. For some people the historic images of Cross and Christ and Father God remain potent, stirring to ways of life and perception and creative of distinctive community. For others these images are dead, as the surge of response to the "death of God" theologies of the 1960s illustrates. There seems no predicting or controlling this phenomenon of the "living" or "dying" of ultimate imagery. Whether myths live or die for given persons or communities is beyond voluntary control and is one of the mysteries we must be prepared to face and accept in our time.

Deeply different imagery, at any rate, is "living" today for many who may be united in the rejection of the scientistic *mythos* and technolatry. For some it may be the biblical world-picture that shapes and expresses their values; for others it may be the imagery of astrology, with mysterious emanations and influences binding the universe of human interests with the universe at large. For others, especially the young, the *mythos* of American Indian culture is living and potent, depicting mankind in gentle animistic relations to the world around us, with shamanistic communication both possible and needed. Charles Reich found many followers for his imagery of a "greening" America in which Consciousness III would rise quietly to perform a greater revolution in our society than politics ever could. Maoists, on the other hand, are sustained by images of human nature and history that permit a world of harmonious and decent life for all through a communist compact that provides justice among all persons and productive intercourse—wooing, not rape—with nature's bounty. Still others, believers in the possibility of a reformed and responsible capitalism, entertain images of the marketing of what may be variously listed as "intermediate technology," "alternative technology," "village technology," "appropriate technology," "people's technology," "organic technology," "ecological technology," "biotechnics," or "soft technology" in place of the large-scale technolatrous corporate technologies of modern times. Erich Fromm combines Marxist and Freudian imagery in his vision of a future society grounded in people-power and in pursuit of *biophilous* ("life-loving") values. Victor Ferkiss offers us a picture of technological mankind living with a new naturalism, or awareness of the dynamic dignity of the environment, a new holism, or realization of how interconnected everything is, and a new immanentism, or openness to finding the sacred not "up there" but close at hand in nature and society. And Robert L. Heilbroner explicitly invokes the "magic" of mythic imagery at the conclusion of *An Inquiry into the Human Prospect,* urging us to rediscover patient Atlas as our spiritual focus in place of nervous and ultimately deadly Prometheus.

These actual and proposed images illustrate some of the multiplicity of basic value-foci that we must expect to live with during this unsettled time of transition, at least. It makes the prospect of a single *mythos* for the bringing in of post-modern consciousness seem rather dim. But one feature in all this variety deserves notice: there does seem to be a gathering consensus, of sorts, if not in terms of the specific value-laden images themselves at least in terms of certain fundamental values that are in distinct contrast to those typical of technolatrous modern consciousness.

These values include the readiness to accept limits and constraints on personal appetites and expectations. Whether these limits are imaged in terms of a concerned Heavenly Father or an astral influence, a personified nature or the larger needs of society, is not the point here. Of main significance is that a basic value is placed on self-control within a finite setting.

These shared values also include the recognition of the integrity or the dignity of the other as a perceived center of intrinsic significance. What limits us is not blind, mechanical necessity, as the deterministic images of objective consciousness tend to depict. Instead, whether it be the needs of the people or the divine will, strangely perceptive plants or meaningful rhythms of organic balance, we are confronted with an Other to which we can relate and which we may respect as having interiority as legitimate and value-centering as our own, though very likely of a different sort. This readiness to value the semiautonomous Other makes possible the renegotiation of Monod's "lost compact" with the universe. The imagery depicting the sort of compact it may be tends to differ greatly, but the practical effect and the moral intent cohere.

If this is so, then despite the unlikelihood of a great cognitive synthesis or a single dominant *mythos* in our time, we are not without the basis for a creative religious response to our historic need. I shall in the remainder of this chapter sketch a spiritual strategy that I shall call Polymythic Organicism, and in the final chapters I shall suggest some ways of applying it toward helping a more desirable future to be born.

II

Polymythic Organicism is a religious posture for those, like me, who find this to be time "between models"—both cognitive and valuational—that might in more settled eras shape a single confident vision of the ultimate. It is a religious stance that affirms as legitimate and exciting the possibility of pluralism in mythic imagery within a context of undergirding fundamental values. It is not a religious response *without* organizing imagery but, rather, one with *many* value-focusing sets of myths welcome within it.

Such a religious posture would necessarily sacrifice the sometimes fanatical power that comes from wholehearted and single-minded involvement within a single grand myth. It would require a tolerance for ambiguity that, to some, would seem a far cry from the fervor that we in the West have frequently associated with religious sincerity. But the other side of such tolerance is liberation: liberation from imprisonment in a single set of images that no longer seems quite large enough for life, and liberation from the parochialism of association and imagination that ties us to the *mythos* of a single community. Polymythic Organicism does not mourn over lost certitudes, but rejoices in the new dimensions of possibility that are open to view.

These new spiritual possibilities, though plural, are not shapeless, of course. Some mythic forms simply do not meet Polymythic Organicism's criterion of appropriateness. The images of unlimited material "progress," for example, or the alienating world-pictures of scientism, or the exclusive preoccupation with the Promethean myth, would be resisted on behalf of fundamental organismic values that make this religious posture take on, for all its mythic pluralism, a definite shape.

This shape reflects certain fundamental features of healthy organic life. At a minimum these would include, first, acknowledgement of the constant balance between growth and death (*anabolism* and *catabolism*) that maintains healthy organisms at proper scale and within finite limits. The miracle of homeostasis, in other words, becomes an object of deep valuation.

Likewise, second, a valued feature of healthy organic life must be the balance between local differentiation of function and holistic mutuality of connection. Even in unicellular organisms we find this balance between differentiation and connectedness; much more strikingly we find it exemplified in the higher, vastly more complex organisms wherein local semiautonomy and the general good coexist harmoniously.

And, third, the balance between necessity and spontaneity will be a valued feature of healthy organic life. Living organisms neither are exempt from the general constraints of physical law nor are they mere flotsam on the causal tide of nature; they have the power of invention, of novel stratagems in response to novel challenge; they have some degree—greater in the higher organisms—of creative self-determinism within the larger determinations of the natural order.

These three features: *homeostasis,* differentiated *holism,* and *creativity,* represent fundamental values for Polymythic Organicism. Drawn from the basic image of healthy life, they are capable of supporting definite attitudes even while remaining hospitably open to a variety of grander mythic exemplifications—Christian, Marxist, Astrological, Shamanistic, and the like—so long as these are suitably interpreted and lived.

In the final chapters of this book I shall attempt to develop an understanding of the primary values of Polymythic Organicism as they may apply to our institutions of religion, education, economics, and politics. First, however, it may be appropriate to expand a bit on what sorts of attitudes, in general, toward our beliefs, toward nature, and toward our fellows, might be associated with this religious strategy for "living the transition" between the modern and the post-modern worlds.

First, Polymythic Organicism demands a sophisticated attitude towards our own belief-systems. We need a revitalized sense of mystery in knowing. At best our cognitive constructs are only that: cognitive constructs. The better they are the more they reveal the mysteries beyond.

I have dwelt enough already in this chapter on the need for a sense of mystery in the sciences. This, it seems to me, should be perceived as a healthy awareness, to be greeted without fear or despair. And it should be perceived as appropriate to all our cognitive constructs—philosophical, political, historical, religious—as well as scientific. Such a perception will lead to a new sense of limits in all our attempts at knowing, and a new readiness to accept those limits without rage and even with joy.

Our beliefs are finite dwelling places for our minds. We

build them as carefully as we can, if we are wise, using the sturdiest materials we can find and then putting them together in the best way we are able. They generally serve us adequately, sustaining and defending us tolerably well. Built spaciously they can house our fellows in great number and can thereby make for civilized community. But it should not shock us that there are other such dwelling places besides ours, or that they will not last forever, or that there are vast domains still outside our highest arching vaults. Even a fine house need not be the only one—or the only type of one. Even a well-constructed house experiences the shocks of weather and the erosion of wear. This means that as we "live the transition" we should school ourselves to be alert to the main alternatives to our own familiar structures, and that we should discipline ourselves to recognize the need for repair, remodeling—or even sometimes moving, since no less finite dwelling places may still be better or worse, larger or smaller, than one another.

Ambiguity need not be destructive or paralyzing, then. It may be liberating and zestful if our attitudes are prepared for it and if our sense of human possibilities is kept wisely in touch with our sense of human finitude. Living the transition to the post-modern world challenges us to such attitudes toward our own beliefs.

Likewise, second, Polymythic Organicism requires a major change in our attitudes toward the natural environment. We need a revitalized sense of the mystery around us. In that sensitivity we shall regain our feeling for the semiautonomous "more" in nature that modern consciousness drove out: "more," that is, than we can fully comprehend in our finite theories of nature, and "more" than we can—or ought—to control for narrow human ends. Such a sense of mystery leads directly, then, to the voluntary acceptance of organismic limits on our treatment of nature. It will require us to accept a broader time-frame for our policies regarding nature. The larger needs of "then" will need to be more heavily weighed in the balance with the parochial wants of "now." But, further, the very control-syndrome itself—the supposition that we have or should aspire to absolute autonomy unbalanced by holistic mutuality, whether in the short term or the long—will need to acknowledge its limits, not out of resignation but out of healthy affirmation of the human situation as properly one of organic partnership with, rather than sheer dominion over, the natural world around us.

For this attitude to be adopted with good will, however, another one is necessary, springing from the voluntary affirmation of homeostatic limits: namely, the acknowledgement of the virtues of thrift, simplicity, or bare sufficiency. As human numbers grow and the earth's resources shrink, the material share we can claim as fairly ours will necessarily diminish with the years ahead. The limits I speak of will be enforced by nature, whether we adopt them gracefully or not; my suggestion is that we seize the moral initiative.

Natural organic limits need not be demoralizing, then. They may spur us to a fuller sense of what besides material consumption constitutes fulfillment in human life. Rather than struggling vainly against the narrowing limits, only to taste the bitter fruit of defeat, we may prepare ourselves now, with dignity, to seek other creative satisfactions. Living the transition to the post-modern world challenges us to newly constructive attitudes toward nature.

Third, and still similarly, Polymythic Organicism requires that we cultivate distinctive attitudes toward our fellow humans. We need a revitalized sense of the mystery in human variety, creativity, and intrinsic worth. There is urgent need to upgrade our respect for the uniqueness, the privileged "insideness," the subjective stubbornness of human individuals. Each of us, is, in principle, hidden in the center of his or her consciousness from all others. We all see the world from our own point of view. There are structural similarities and holistic connections, of course, or there could be no language, no community, no distinctively human life. But it is also distinctively human to

have a certain opaqueness all one's own—the mystery of
"me," *my* being, *my* values, *my* birth, *my* death, *my*
purposes, *my* creative spontaneity.

In this sense of mystery in dealing with fellow human
beings, we shall find the attitudinal basis for the voluntary
acceptance of limits, yet again. One of our limits will be felt at
the point where we have been accustomed to manipulating
other persons. Whether in large numbers or singly, whether for
benevolent motives or for selfish ones, the one-way
manipulative, controlling attitude is wrong from the viewpoint
of Polymythic Organicism. Technologies of behavior, however
well intended, belong to the technolatrous frame of mind.
They neglect the precious, mysterious, interior of the persons
being controlled. They neglect the creative inventiveness of
healthy organic life as well as the proper organic mutuality in
holistic controls. What I earlier called the control-syndrome is
what has brought modern mankind to its present parlous
condition: we feel we must unilaterally control every aspect of
nature to maximize our wealth; thus we must control our
wealth to enjoy it; thus we must control our neighbor so that
he or she will not steal from us; thus we must control the
society to preserve our privileges; thus we must control world
markets and resources so that our society will prosper; thus we
must control a military establishment capable of controlling the
covetous (or hostile, etc.) impulses of other societies who also
have military establishments aimed at controlling our similar
impulses; thus we must control the balance of terror . . . if we
can! And so it goes, to competition and to war. Unchecked by
recognition of the mysterious dignity of others and the need
for real mutuality, the control-syndrome leads to disaster. *Self*-
limitation, in contrast, is always in the context of our
subjective recognition of the dignity and freedom of our own
selfhood. The dangers of living the transition require much
more of the latter (voluntary limitation) and much less of the
former (manipulation of others).

Equally, the healthy sense of mystery in other personal

centers of experience and value will place limits on our expectation of mythological uniformity. The possibilities of pluralism will be accepted as natural and less threatening. The rich variety of the world may be more cheerfully embraced. We may celebrate our differences rather than attack each other, given these attitudes.

Self-limitation in dealing with other persons need not be demeaning, then. It may be evocative of new, creative social patterns based on mutual respect rather than mistrust, competition, conformity, and manipulation. Living the transition to the post-modern world challenges us to fresh, reconciling attitudes toward our fellows.

This survey of attitudes illustrates the general value stance represented by Polymythic Organicism, especially as these translate into an ethic for living the transition. But an ethic is not a whole religion. If Polymythic Organicism adopts such a hospitable attitude toward a *variety* of mythic models, is it not the equivalent of living *without* myths? I suspect that for many the demands of pluralistic openness will be too heavy to maintain; and for them a single religious *mythos* may be needed for valuational and intellectual wholeness. As long as the religious imagery adopted is compatible with the basic post-modern values we have seen to be needed no harm is done, though some of the excitement and richness of pluralism is lost.

For others, however, none of the available myths may be "living" to the degree that wholehearted commitment is possible without hypocrisy. If so, perhaps something I wrote exactly a decade ago for the concluding pages of my *Basic Modern Philosophy of Religion* may be helpful here:

> For those who find themselves in this position . . . it may become necessary to learn how to live without religious models. But this is not the same as abandoning all responsible religion. If my general view of religion has merit, a person's religion is not constituted first of all by his allegiance to imagery but rather by his

most comprehensive and intensive valuations. A religious life without [commitment to a single set of] imagery is no contradiction, therefore, though I suppose that it must be prepared to sacrifice the help such imagery provides in achieving the practical and theoretical interconnections called for by the ideal of coherence. To this extent, then, it will also be handicapped in attaining the sense of understanding that might be hoped for. But despite this I must confess that the present moment seems to be a time "between models" for me and for many others, a time when we are required to acknowledge our nakedness with whatever rueful dignity we can muster and admit that despite our cravings— of which we need not be ashamed—we do not understand as well as we might wish.

Living with partial meanings and "broken myths" is one thing; but must this then not exclude the possibility of anything like a rich religious life? Must a life "between models" be parched and shallow, without the heights of worship, the depths of prayer, the breadth of fellowship? So it is often assumed, but I believe otherwise.

At its most general, and aside from the particulars with which it is always concretely found, worship is the unlimited adoration, through whatever forms are taken to be appropriate, of whatever is held to be "sacred," i.e., whatever is valued beyond everything else as most pressingly important and most unavoidably relevant. There is no special posture, no special location essential to worship in this sense. Standing in a picket line may be as much an exalting act of worship as kneeling in a cathedral. I frankly admit that teaching or writing philosophy are, for me, sometimes sacred acts.

Likewise prayer, the aspect of worship involving the conscious entertainment in thought and affirmation in will of the sacred, is not necessarily forfeit for those who must live "between models." On the contrary, everyone who cares deeply about his values both can and should pause to reaffirm, from time to time, his basic priorities. Philosophers and prophets alike warn us that from the distractions and compromises of our daily pursuits we need to withdraw and regain perspective. Philosophers are inclined to call this movement "contemplation"; prophets call it prayer. If the model of a particular religion has a personal focus in God, as is familiar in Western civilization, it is quite natural that prayers will take the form (often, though not always) of personal address. But this, as is evident from any study of world religions, is not essential to prayer. What is essential in mature prayer[8] is the affirmation, however it may be symbolized, of a value-ordering that, whether manifested well or badly in daily affairs, remains normative for one's life. Think for a moment of the types of prayer: the acknowledgment of the (inevitable) gap between profession and practice is the heart of all "penitential" prayer; the focus upon and celebration of supreme values is the basis for "prayers of thanksgiving"; and even where a personal model permits "petitionary" prayer, sophisticated theists have never approved the shopping list approach to God. For Christians the model petitionary prayer is: "Thy will be done." Thus prayer, rightly understood, does not need to be demeaning or superstitious. Without a theistic model it is still possible, I believe, to breathe the equivalent of "Thy will be done": i.e., "May those values that I acknowledge as really sacred, beyond the petty and inconstant willfulness of my momentary desires, find genuine fulfillment." "Thy Kingdom come!" Religious imagery may make one's priorities concrete and vivid, but this is not logically or psychologically necessary for prayer at its most essential level.

What, finally, of fellowship? Must a life "between models" sacrifice the community of shared allegiances that is one of the key benefits of organized religion? In part, I fear, this may be necessary. At present the commonly available institutional religious alternatives do seem to me, at least, to involve imagery articulated by theories that are not honestly affirmable. And so we who cannot participate are cut off by the demand for basic integrity, as we see it, from the offer of such community extended on those conditions.

Men can share basic values, however, without belonging to the same institutions or giving assent to the same images. Perhaps—my analysis of religion suggests this optimistic possibility—sharing basic values, even without sharing traditional ideational forms, is what constitutes sharing a common religion. To this extent we who are on the outside of institutional religion may continue to find meaningful fellowship with others of good will, even apart from the traditional formulas that personal integrity forbids. Is this fellowship important? Indeed it is. "Integrity," after all is a poverty-stricken term if it forces a man to shrink into an "integer," standing isolated and apart from other men. It makes all the difference what one's integrity "integrates" into one's life. The ideal kind of integrity, as I have urged in the course of my argument, would make possible wholeness based on some principle that could both give unity to oneself and bring various selves into ever richer, ever widening unities. A wholeness that is always open, a unity that, by its very nature, is hospitable to growth—this is what is needed as the basis for religious maturity and life's fullest integrity.

The organismic virtues of rich differentiation within the balanced limits of unity are what we fundamentally seek in our post-modern world. Richness and wholeness, variety and integrity in mutual community, is what Polymythic Organicism is all about. Can such a spiritual vision, generating such ethical attitudes, be fruitfully related to our turbulent transitional world? The final part of this book will attempt to supply some needed connections.

Notes

1. William G. Pollard, *The Mystery of Matter (United States Atomic Energy Commission, Office of Information Services, 1974), p. 54.*
2. *Ibid., p. 50.*
3. *Gunther S. Stent, The Coming of the Golden Age: A View of the End of Progress* (Garden City, N.Y.: Natural History Press, 1969), p. 64.
4. Ibid., p. 65.
5. *See,* William G. Pollard, "The Language of Life" (Paper delivered at the Conference on Science and Technology and Their Impact on Modern Society, Herceq Novi, Yugoslavia, Sept. 16–23, 1964), esp. p. 12.
6. Barry Commoner, *Saturday Review,* 1 October 1966, p. 75.
7. Harold K. Schilling, *The New Consciousness in Science and Religion* (Philadelphia: United Church Press, 1973), p. 45.
8. All developed religious traditions permit qualitative judgments about degrees of adequacy or maturity in prayer.

III
HELPING THE FUTURE
TO BE BORN

7. HOPE IN RELIGIOUS INSTITUTIONS

One of the ironies I have noticed in our present situation is that many people in the universities who have never had much personal use for institutional religion are now rediscovering the churches and synagogues with a vengeance. Not for themselves, of course, but as engines of social change for the masses whose consciousness and ethical sensibilities need instant reform in the current ecological and historical crises that threaten us.

I

I have been struck at the numbers of my students in Environmental Studies who have hit upon this "solution" to society's ills. After becoming aware of the urgent need for a new consciousness in our time, they first tend to think in terms of spreading this new gospel through the mass communications media: a great blitz campaign over television and radio, magazines and newspapers, in support of a gentler, less frantically consuming, more organically restrained mode of life and thought. But then the thought usually strikes them that Marshall McLuhan would laugh, and rightly so, at such an enterprise. If ever his slogan "the medium is the message" can be clearly illustrated, it is through the intimate connection between our modern mass media and our modern mass society. The modern exploitative, manipulative, materialist, unrestrained, growth-obsessed consciousness is nowhere better studied than in our typical media. Modern consciousness at its most objectionable *is* their primary message. To expect these media to take the lead in ushering in a radically opposed post-modern consciousness, my students generally conclude, is ludicrous. Even if there were no moral qualms about the blatant mass manipulation of minds that would be involved (and there are plenty of such qualms), the commercial pressures that control the media would never permit such a commercially suicidal blitz campaign to occur. "Who would pay for it?" is the bottom-line comment on that suggestion.

Next my students often propose that education is the answer. The means, at least, would be compatible with the end (though in some school systems one might well wonder even about that); but this proposal has evident defects as well. Institutionalized education, unlike mass propaganda, is too slow a process to meet the urgent timetable on which our survival may depend. Besides, education of the scope and depth required would remain an exercise for the elite. Ours is a historical challenge in which all are involved and in which great changes of value and perception must occur generally. The presence or absence of institutional educational credentials cannot be the distinguishing mark for healthful post-modern consciousness if our society as a whole is to live the transition successfully.

Thus institutional religion is rediscovered. Looked at from outside it seems to be the perfect instrument for needed value changes in society at large. The institutions are all in place; they do not have to be specially invented or paid for. They are supported and attended by a complete cross section of society; a mass audience is promised. They are not obviously controlled by commercial interests; they should be able to strike an independent note against the current powers that be. And, best of all, they already deal with values before a believing group ready to accept on faith what is preached and sung. Pictured as somewhere between the media of mass propaganda and elitist educational institutions, the churches and synagogues raise the flagging hopes of those in search of a needed engine of social change.

I have had intimate dealings with institutional religion all my life, and so my hopes (though real, as I shall show below) must be more moderate. Even the metaphor of the churches as "engine" for social change strikes me as brash. As an airplane pilot I tend to think of engines as very important features indeed! They are generally out in front; they are as powerful as they are noisy; their pull makes all the difference. Perhaps the institutionalized religions were once potent enough to merit such a metaphor, but surely this is the case no longer. The real motivating forces, the active engines in our society are the other, often unrecognized religious realities of technolatry and objective consciousness, including their manifestations in economics and politics. The churches, more realistically, are just along for the ride.

Is this excessively harsh? I have tried to think of other more appropriate metaphors for institutional religion's place on fuselage of modern society. If not the engine, then are the churches the rudder—at the tail end of things but still functional? Perhaps this is a better image, since in flight the rudder really doesn't steer (the ailerons do that) but simply keeps the turns coordinated. I had contemplated proposing the metaphor of the humble trim tab, but this seems unduly diminishing of the churches' role, not least since the setting of the trim tab is usually only noticed in straight-and-level flight. The rudder is a better image, especially since there are times, especially at crucial moments, when it is vital to perform *un*-coordinated maneuvers; at such times the influence of a cross-controllable rudder is enormously important; in forcing itself stubbornly against the normal wind-flow, by creating drag and turbulence (even at the tail end) it may save the whole craft in a cross-wind situation.

To extend this metaphor one more degree: our modern society is on final approach to the post-modern world. The turbulence is terrific and due to get more severe. The shifting cross winds are fierce and dangerous. The churches are not the engines speeding our craft along toward doom or happy landings, but they may have a crucial influence—if only by disturbing the normal flow of the slipstream generated by our rush toward destiny. In the sections to follow I shall show some of the ways that Judaism and Christianity, our primary institutional religions, may play the stubborn rudder's role.

II

A fuller discussion of Judaism would need to recognize the extent to which different strands and traditions exist side by side, with different emphases and interpretations. My brief treatment, which is meant merely to be suggestive of the values that Polymythic Organicism would commend and reinforce in the general Judaic *mythos,* will have to ignore this finer texture, though it is important for actual institutional Judaism and I hope that others will be stimulated to work out the details for specific application.

One of the ways in which Jewish consciousness has been most in contrast to the typical modern mind—one of the sources of the felt "differentness" that has often contributed to the sense of Jews as alien in the modern world—is the readiness to live under ritual restraints. In the previous chapter I identified one of the basic values of organicism as self-limitation: maintenance of balance, homeostasis. Cancers and bacterial cultures grow heedlessly until external limits force an end to such life; healthy organisms have inbuilt means of maintaining scale and due proportion. Any desirable post-modern consciousness will need to provide the basis for the voluntary acceptance of limits, and here Judaism's *observant attitude* may be of historic importance. Not all Jewish families are equally "observant," of course; not all Jewish denominations require the same specific observances of their faithful. But deep in the fabric of Judaism itself remains the recognition that human beings live under authority; that not all things are permitted; and that to observe the Law of God is the faithful Jew's first duty. Life under the restraint of law, symbolized variously in daily acts of self-limitation, is at the center of historic Jewish consciousness.

There is no guarantee that an observant attitude in one part of life will bring about restraint in all parts, economic as well as ritualistic. The prophetic thunder within Judaism has rumbled again and again against the failure of ritual observance to follow through in ethical practice.

> I hate, I despise your feasts, and I will take no delight in your solemn assemblies. Yea, though ye offer me your burnt-offerings and meal-offerings, I will not accept them; neither will I regard the peace-offerings of your fat beasts. Take thou away from me the noise of thy songs; for I will not hear the melody of thy viols. But let justice roll down as waters, and righteousness as a mighty stream (Amos 5:21–24 ASV).

But the cultivation of an observant attitude toward life, though not all that is needed in an adequate post-modern consciousness, is an important advance over the distinctly unobservant attitudes of modernity. Jewish observant consciousness provides a basis for voluntary acceptance of limits, for restraints on the progressive hubris that has characterized our society's spiritual life, and for the homeostasis that we must learn to maintain if we are to live the transition to a new social order in dignity and health.

A second fundamental value of Polymythic Organicism is based on the holistic interconnectedness of healthy life. There is differentiation at all levels, but always within a context of unity. Here Judaism deeply reinforces organismic consciousness both in its basic imagery regarding human beings and in its venerable attitudes toward the land and all the creatures living upon it.

Men and women are not shown, in the Genesis myths (which Jews have tended to interpret somewhat differently from Hellenized Christians who share the same stories), as radically different beings from the rest of nature. There is differentiation of function, but no destruction of the holism in nature's web. The dust of the earth is the stuff of human form, and breath is the secret of life. The mind-body (or soul-body) problem that has plagued philosophy since the ancient Greeks is not a difficulty within classical Jewish thought since the philosophically postulated different substances, mind-stuff and body-stuff, are not part of Judaic imagery. The problem of finding connections is outflanked at the start by a holistic vision in which the living human body is not a composite of two unlike realities but, rather, a unity of animate flesh.

Similarly, human intercourse with the land and all its creatures remain holistic though differentiated. One's land is not absolute property to do with as one pleases. The observant attitude requires restraints and a sense of mutuality for the sake of the poor, for the sake of the animals who live and work on the land, and for the sake of the land itself. Land, for example, is not supposed to be exploited to the maximum degree at the time of harvest. Deuteronomic law at one point justifies such restraint on the basis of concern for the poor and powerless:

> When thou reapest thy harvest in thy field, and hast forgot a sheaf in the field, thou shalt not go again to fetch it: it shall be for the sojourner, for the fatherless, and for the widow; that Jehovah thy God may bless thee in all the work of thy hands. When thou beatest thine olive-tree, thou shalt not go over the boughs again: it shall be for the sojourner, for the fatherless, and for the widow. When thou gatherest the grapes of thy vineyard, thou shalt not glean it after thee: it shall be for the sojourner, for the fatherless, and for the widow. And thou shalt remember that thou wast a

bondman in the land of Egypt: therefore I command thee to do this thing (Deut. 24:19–22 ASV).

Such consideration is not reserved for powerless human beings alone, however, since the same sort of protection is extended in the same context to the beasts of the field. Ignoring all economic interest, which would argue *against* sharing one's harvest beyond minimum necessity with the working animals, Deuteronomic law commands: "Thou shalt not muzzle the ox when he treadeth out the grain" (Deut. 24:4 ASV). Not muzzle the ox! He will be sure to help himself generously, with temptation placed so near. Yes, but the holistic sense of mutual connection to the animals with whom we live and work demands that we woo rather than rape. There is differentiation between the farmer and his oxen, but the proper organic relation involves mutuality, not mere exploitation.

Even the cropland itself is not mere property, to be used to the maximum without regard or restraint. The rights of sabbath rest are extended also to the fields by the Levitical commandment:

> Six years thou shalt sow thy field, and six years thou shalt prune thy vineyard, and gather in the fruits thereof; but in the seventh year shall be a sabbath of solemn rest for the land, a sabbath unto Jehovah: thou shalt neither sow thy field, nor prune thy vineyard. That which groweth of itself of thy harvest thou shalt not reap, and the grapes of thy undressed vine thou shalt not gather: it shall be a year of solemn rest for the land (Lev. 25:3–5 ASV).

Nor is sabbath rest the only consideration due the sustaining land on which mankind gratefully dwells. Leviticus imposes a requirement which, if observed, would forbid the permanent commercialization of our natural heritage. After seven sabbaths of rest for the land, or forty-nine years, comes the Jubilee year in which not only persons who have fallen into slavery but also land that has been bought and sold are to be given their freedom again.

> And ye shall hallow the fiftieth year, and proclaim liberty
> throughout the land unto all the inhabitants thereof: it shall be a
> jubilee unto you; and ye shall return every man unto his possession
> and ye shall return every man unto his family. . . . And the land
> shall not be sold in perpetuity; for the land is mine: for ye are
> strangers and sojourners with me (Lev. 25:10, 23 ASV).

The land is not to be reduced to mere "real estate," then, in
this paradigm of holistic consciousness toward nature. Neither
people nor pastures are to be sold into permanent slavery.
Jewish thought at this point has touched a profound theme of
organicism and offers an important element in a viable
post-modern consciousness.

Finally, Polymythic Organicism values what I called the
intrinsic dignity of creative self-determinism in healthy
organisms. People have purposes. They have an inwardness, a
for-itself status that deserves respect. Domination of the poor
by the rich, or of the unfortunate by the high and mighty, is
morally repulsive. Jewish thought is keenly aware of the need
for restraint against what I earlier called the "control
syndrome," which so easily slips into callous manipulation and
injustice. The larger prophetic tradition, which is deep and
central to Judaism, demands economic justice, then, within a
framework of holistic respect for nature and obedience to
God.

Domination itself is morally indivisible. As Deuteronomy and
Leviticus suggest, domination of every last sheaf in one's field
is related to domination over the friendless sojourner or the
defenseless widow; domination of the draft animals on the
land is related to domination over the earth itself. The Jewish
prophetic tradition extends this concept pointedly, and modern
Judaism is in a position to recognize the extent to which the
tools and institutions of the modern world have permitted us
of the modern world to dominate, unjustly and unequally, the
resources of the planet. The keen social conscience of an
Amos linked to a similar awareness of current events today

will quickly uncover the extent to which privilege and greed are perpetuated by the techniques and structures of our modern society itself, the extent to which judgment is merited upon the dominating societies of the earth, and the ways in which redemptive social policies might painfully but urgently be put into effect. These insights are among the most needed for the times of transition that are upon us. The resources of the Jewish prophetic tradition in providing moral clarification for our turbulent age are much needed.

Needed also is the prophetic vision of the new world that longs to arise. Such visions of the ideal inspire and lure even as the prophetic ethical lash drives and pushes. Beyond domination and injustice lies the messianic promise of a society, under God, in harmony with itself and with the universe. Perhaps the best example of such a vision was authored by Isaiah:

> And his delight shall be in the fear of Jehovah; and he shall not judge after the sight of his eyes, neither decide after the hearing of his ears; but with righteousness shall he judge the poor, and decide with equity for the meek of the earth; and he shall smite the earth with the rod of his mouth; and with the breath of his lips shall he slay the wicked. And righteousness shall be the girdle of his waist, and faithfulness the girdle of his loins.
>
> And the wolf shall dwell with the lamb, and the leopard shall lie down with the kid; and the calf and the young lion and the fatling together; and a little child shall lead them. And the cow and the bear shall feed; their young ones shall lie down together; and the lion shall eat straw like the ox. And the sucking child shall play on the hole of the asp, and the weaned child shall put his hand on the adder's den. They shall not hurt nor destroy in all my holy mountain; for the earth shall be full of the knowledge of Jehovah, as the waters cover the sea (Isa. 11:3–9 ASV).

Here is a beautiful dream of a magical world quite unlike our own. It is a dream of integrity and wholeness, in contrast to the dualism between ruler and ruled, man and nature, world and God. It is a dream of harmony, in contrast to the ruthless pursuit of profit, domination, and control. And it is a dream of justice, in contrast to the inequalities and torments of our world. It is a dream well worth the dreaming. It summarizes the contributions to post-modern consciousness that may be hoped for from Judaism. In this dream we see how gladly we could welcome the Judaizing of modern consciousness for the humanizing of the world. It is a dream that forces itself out against the slipstream from our current path; in this way the *mythos* of Judaism may help us make our needed turn.

III

Christianity, too, offers grounds for hope as an instrument of constructive consciousness change. Even short of the extensive theological reforms that I discussed previously in chapter 5, Christianity in the churches as they exist today provides the leverage points, if they will be used, for significant assistance in changing the mind of the modern world. As in my treatment of Judaism, specific variations growing out of the multiplicity of traditions, denominations, and sects will need to be supplied elsewhere; I shall focus on central traits, again, that from the perspective of Polymythic Organicism are clearly to be appreciated. The following is not intended as a balanced critique of Christianity, then, but as a few suggestions—for those outside as well as inside the churches—about how historic Christianity may be perceived as a current resource in living the transition to the post-modern world.

The need for learning to live with limits, which we have noted as one of the primary requirements of our time, is deeply embedded in historic Christianity. Homeostasis is nothing alien to a religion founded on reverence for the humble Carpenter from rural Palestine. The roots of Christian faith are deep in the lower classes of the Hellenistic world, where poverty and slavery were no strangers. There has been an antimaterialist note in Christianity from the beginning:

> And he said unto them, take heed, and keep yourselves from all
> covetousness: for a man's life consisteth not in the abundance of

the things which he possesseth. And he spake a parable unto them, saying, the ground of a certain rich man brought forth plentifully: and he reasoned within himself, saying, What shall I do, because I have not where to bestow my fruits? And he said, This will I do: I will pull down my barns, and build greater; and there will I bestow all my grain and my goods. And I will say to my soul, Soul thou hast much goods laid up for many years; take thine ease, eat, drink, be merry. But God said unto him, Thou foolish one, this night is thy soul required of thee; and the things thou hast prepared, whose shall they be? So is he that layeth up treasure for himself, and is not rich toward God (Luke 12:15–21 ASV).

Despite the sumptuousness of some churches in some periods of Christendom, Christian faith has never abandoned—in principle—its antimaterialist heritage. The vows of poverty taken by many clergy are reminders that material simplicity is an honorable estate. This is not a popular theme in modern churches, nor is it widely practiced, but it should not be forgotten since it is deeply embedded in the Christian *mythos* and is potentially a recoverable resource for demanding times. Christianity need not be embarrassed, at least, by the need for a whole society to limit its material consumption and expectations: it has something constructive to say to the situation.

Another urgent point of self-limitation, as we have seen, is with regard to population. Christianity has by no means played a constructive role, worldwide, in the controversies over contraception. But despite all the polemics, it has never been the Christian position that people should breed mindlessly, like rabbits. Even the staunchest opponent of artificial birth control, Pope Paul, recognizes the "licitness" of avoiding pregnancies under many circumstances; his wrath is directed against the technical hubris and "illicit" means by which these licit ends may be sought. I have no intention of defending the papal stand on birth control, which has posed a grave problem of conscience for many within the Roman Catholic church, but it should be recognized that all Christians—including even the Pope—acknowledge the appropriately voluntary nature of human reproduction. Sexuality has always been perceived as a matter of choice, not fate. Jesus, as far as we know, did not marry or have offspring. St. Paul, likewise, recommends the celibate life for those who are strong enough to take it. The vows of chastity taken by many clergy over many ages are reminders that Christianity puts human reproduction in a larger context of moral control. In my view it is not enough, given the threat to civilization itself posed by the exponential curves of human population growth, to rely on unaided "chastity" as the sole licit means of exercising that moral control. "New occasions teach new duties," as the famous hymn proclaims. But within an appropriate understanding of the moral requirements of our time, Christianity's fundamentally voluntarist attitude toward sexuality and reproduction is a resource for living with the constraints that will be necessary to accept in the post-modern world.

Besides recognizing the value of constraints, Polymythic Organicism urges the need for holism, we recall, in relations among human beings and between humanity and nature. In the context of this need it is interesting to note the abundance of organic figures of speech that are employed in central places in the New Testament depicting the proper relationships for Christians with Christ and with each other. In one of the great climactic passages in the Gospel of John, Jesus adopts an organic metaphor:

> I am the true vine, and my Father is the husbandman. Every branch in me that beareth not fruit, he taketh it away: and every branch that beareth fruit, he cleanseth it, that it may bear more fruit. Already ye are clean because of the word which I have spoken unto you. Abide in me, and I in you. As the branch cannot bear fruit of itself, except it abide in the vine; so neither can ye, except ye abide in me. I am the vine, ye are the branches: He that abideth in me, and I in him, the same beareth much fruit: for apart from me ye can do nothing (John 15:1–5 ASV).

The image of mutual "abiding" through organic holism is echoed by St. Paul on more than one occasion. Writing to the Romans, he compares the young Christian community to an organism that has local diversification within an overall unity.

> For even as we have many members in one body, and all the members have not the same office: so we, who are many, are one body in Christ, and severally members one of another. And having gifts differing according to the grace that was given to us, whether prophecy, let us prophesy according to the proportion of our faith; or ministry, let us give ourselves to our ministry; or he that teacheth, to his teaching; or he that exhorteth, to his exhorting: he that giveth, let him do it with liberality; he that ruleth, with diligence; he that showeth mercy, with cheerfulness (Rom. 12:4–8 ASV).

And in rebuking the Christians at Corinth for petty jealousies that ought not to exist within a community of organic mutuality, St. Paul goes into yet greater detail.

> For as the body is one, and hath many members, and all the members of the body, being many, are one body; so also is Christ. For in one Spirit were we all baptized into one body, whether Jews or Greeks, whether bond or free; and were all made to drink of one Spirit. For the body is not one member, but many. If the foot shall say, Because I am not the hand, I am not of the body; it is not therefore not of the body. And if the ear shall say, Because I am not the eye, I am not of the body; it is not therefore not of the body. If the whole body were an eye, where were the hearing? If the whole were hearing, where were the smelling? But now hath God set the members each one of them in the body, even as it pleased him. And if they were all one member, where were the body? But now they are many members, but one body. And the eye cannot say to the hand, I have no need of thee: or again the head to the feet, I have no need of you. . . . And whether one member suffereth, all the members suffer with it; or one member is honored, all the members rejoice with it. Now ye are the body of Christ, and severally members thereof (I Cor. 12:12–21, 26–27 ASV).

These metaphors are important for Christianity, because they are the images underlying the Christian ideal of community. It is clearly the ideal of differentiation and mutuality, fellowship hospitable to variety, richness held together in wholeness. It is a worthy ideal of human relationships for a more holistic post-modern world.

There is less explicit attention paid to the relations between humanity and the rest of nature in the New Testament. But the imagery we find takes for granted an intimacy that is fully in keeping with the holistic values of Polymythic Organicism. Jesus takes nature as the manifest model of God's concern for all his creatures, reminds his disciples that we are all enveloped in the same concern just as we are all fellow creatures, and urges that human behavior be more natural, less anxious and alienatingly defensive about our material needs. God knows that we have such needs; after all, we are creatures along with all the other creatures that he cares for. Not all creatures need to be credited with equal importance in God's eyes—there is, after all, differentiation within unity—but even the least have some importance, and human importance takes its place on that continuous scale.

> And he said unto his disciples, Therefore I say unto you, Be not anxious for your life, what ye shall eat; nor yet for your body, what ye shall put on. For the life is more than the food, and the body than the raiment. Consider the ravens, that they sow not, neither reap; which have no store-chamber nor barn; and God feedeth them: of how much more value are ye than the birds! And which of you by being anxious can add a cubit unto the measure of his life? If then ye are not able to do even that which is least, why are ye anxious concerning the rest? Consider the lilies, how they grow: they toil not, neither do they spin; yet I say unto you, Even Solomon in all his glory was not arrayed like one of these. But if God doth so clothe the grass in the field, which to-day is, and to-morrow is cast into the oven; how much more shall he clothe you, O ye of little faith? (Luke 12:22–28 ASV).

In this posture of relaxed acceptance of nature and the human place in it, we see a Christian theme that could assist our

civilization in finding a healthier relationship to the
environment.

The third great value insisted on by Polymythic Organicism
is respect for the intrinsic value of the other, as a center of
potential creativity and purpose. Christianity offers support for
such a value at two levels: both in terms of its condemnation
of the distortion of moral relationships, and in terms of its
characteristic ethic of love.

Judgment for sin is one of the crucial themes within
Christian faith. Sin is a state of estrangement from God brought
about by breaking relationships through pride or
self-centeredness of other sorts. In a great Christian image
drawn by St. Paul, nature and mankind both are seen as
suffering from this state of estrangement. In Adam's
disobedience to God, the estrangement began; but with the
basic relationship broken, all others are distorted as well,
including those toward nature. Our abuse of the natural order,
on this Christian vision, is part of our sinful condition.
Disregard for the other in every domain stems from this
defective condition and will be met with just punishment.

It is true, certainly, that modern civilization has manifested
disregard for the Other, both human and environmental; we
have, in Christian language, sinned against humanity and
nature. One of the churches' contributions, unpleasant though
it may be to hear, could be to help us face up to the
seriousness of our estrangement and prepare ourselves
spiritually for the pain of punishment and the labors of
penitential restitution. Judgment is a hard word to hear, and in
late modern times (especially in the "better" churches) the
theme of judgment has been more softly spoken than have
words of blessed assurance. But the days of transition are
bound to be stormy and hard. Modern civilization has sinned
against our fellows, our future, and the earth; the sin is
returning, whether we like it or not, in heavy judgment.
Modern humanity owes a great debt to nature, and this debt
will somehow be repaid. The paying will be a time of anguish.

But Christianity can, if it will, help interpret the moral appropriateness of judgment and help to shape constructive spiritual attitudes toward the pain to come—attitudes of humility, repentance, and a greater awareness both of where the basic spiritual flaw lay and of the proper acts of contrition and repayment.

The other characteristic way in which Christianity supports the valuing of the other is more gentle, but in some ways equally difficult to hear. The central demand of Christian faith is for love—whether we like it or not! The paradox of *agape,* or Christian concern, is that it is commanded. Love is usually thought of as a paradigm of something that operates by inclination alone, but Christian *agape* is intended to rule and shape inclination, not the reverse. In this we see that *agape* is different from the usual sort of love, *eros,* that begins with a need or desire within the self and attempts (as Plato shows in the *Symposium*) to attach the attractive beloved to the yearning self. On the contrary, *agape* is focused on the other's well-being even if the other is not at all attractive. *Agape* grounds an intentional consciousness in which the "intent" is turned wholly toward the object of concern. *Agape* is a giving love, whether there is anything to be gotten back or not. It is the sort of gift that God is, when, without anything to gain for himself, he sets the drama of the Incarnation into being.

> For God so loved the world, that he gave his only begotten Son, that whosoever believeth on him should not perish, but have eternal life. For God sent not the Son into the world to judge the world; but that the world should be saved through him (John 3:16–17 ASV).

If Christianity is true to its own center, *agape,* it will teach its followers how to look for and respect, in thought and deed, the precious otherness that the world supplies. At a minimum this will apply to the otherness of persons—all persons, near or far, friend or foe—toward whom concerned respect will be forthcoming. Maximally, perhaps, Christian *agape* will extend its range from the human and divine into the realm of nature, too. Some Christians have shown the way. St. Francis, with his fraternal attitudes toward all fellow creatures, and Albert Schweitzer, with his "reverence for life," are two notable examples of lovers who do not stop with loving people alone.

In these ways, then, Christianity may be seen as a potential resource for the spiritual needs of the post-modern world. The churches, if they will, may give significant assistance to the birth and nurture of a more desirable post-modern world. There is hope that Christianity may yet play the needed role of stubborn rudder in our passage through the turbulence of these transitionary times.

IV

But will institutional religion actually stiffen itself against the primary windstream of our culture to perform this important role? I feel keenly the hypothetical qualifications one always needs to add toward the end of these discussions: "*If* Christianity is true to its own center . . . ," or "The churches, *if* they will . . ."

No one can answer this question with assurance. In the old language: "Only God knows." But it is possible to distinguish some of the conditions under which these hopes might be met.

First, if Judaism and Christianity are to make a major difference to the course of our civilization, the multiplicity of institutions that are the actual vehicles of those faiths will need to learn how better to coordinate themselves. There is need for a deeper ecumenicity than ever before: not only within the various organized religions, and not only between them, but also among all mythic traditions that share in supporting the life-bringing values needed for the post-modern world. This need is not merely a reflection of the ideology of Polymythic Organicism; it is a requirement of practical effectiveness.

In the third quarter of the twentieth century, some real progress was made toward effective ecumenicity. The World

Council of Churches, mainly Protestant, was and is a phenomenon of real importance. At the doctrinal level there is little movement toward unity; I have participated in the elaborate waltzes of theological courtesy and conflict, and have felt the frustrations that come from dealing at this level with those who are locked single-mindedly and unambiguously into hard-line interpretations of monovalent myths. But at other levels, where the commissions of the World Council operate closer to the domain of applied values, the benefits of differentiation within increasing unity are beginning to be realized. Readers of this book will take special interest in the activities of the Commission on Church and Society, with headquarters in Geneva, Switzerland. Among the activities of this agency of the World Council of Churches is the sponsoring of a series of ecumenical conferences and the publication of a number of papers dealing with Christian social thought in future perspective. An especially interesting series devoted to "The Future of Man and Society in a World of Science-Based Technology," is available through the journal *Anticipation.** Similar movements and activities have taken place under Roman Catholic sponsorship since the Vatican II Council opened that church wider to current breezes; and intra-Jewish cooperative activities, especially with emphasis on social issues, have continued.

Such movement toward religious coordination, though real, is only the beginning of what is needed for our time of transition. The post-modern world cannot afford the starchy exclusivism that still remains the rule within the various institutional traditions. Myths increasingly need to be recognized as myths, and theoretical constructs as theoretical constructs, without anxiety or felt diminution of their importance. The primary values underlying great myths and constructs need more explicit clarification and reassertion

---

Anticipation is published by Church and Society, World Council of Churches, 150 Route de Ferney, 1211 Geneva 20, Switzerland.

within the context of creative pluralism. Pluralism of image, powered by firm commitment to underlying life-bringing values, needs to extend beyond the boundaries of Protestantism or Roman Catholicism or Judaism into every religious expression fit for the organic needs of the post-modern world.

At this point, if this book were not self-limited to our Western heritage (as I promised at the start of part 2), I would want to enter a discussion of Polymythic Organicism and Hinduism, Buddhism, Taoism, Jainism, Islam, and other major religious traditions of the world. They have much in common, seen from the organismic perspective, with our own major faiths, and in the long run they will need to be drawn into a fruitful differentiated unity that sees beyond contrasting mythic styles.

Ecumenism pushed to such a degree will not be easy for the leaders of the institutions that have grown strong on separation. Some religious institutions seem to justify their very existence on the basis of their differences from other institutions, rather than on the basis of their common contributions to the upholding of ultimate values. Therefore it will require unprecedented humility on the part of the leadership, unprecedented flexibility on the part of the laity, and unprecedented good will on the part of all concerned to bring about the concerted effort that will be needed for effective change in the consciousness and the course of our civilization.

Is such unprecedented response likely to be made? The discussion of the first need leads us to notice a second, even more basic, need: the purification and inspiration of the institutional religions themselves. Who are the people on whom our hope for religious assistance rests? Are they somehow different from the rest of us? Have they a special leverage that the rest of us lack?

As to who the people are who make up the religious institutions around us, we know the answer: they are by and large simply the ordinary people of our culture. They are indeed, as my students see, a cross section of the population, for better or for worse. Consequently, the churches and synagogues are mainly in the hands of adherents to the average values of the modern world. We see this illustrated in every direction: in the insistence of one congregation on installing a new air-conditioning plant for its sanctuary, despite known energy shortages and desperate human need; or in the pride taken by another parish in the canny investment of its building fund in growth securities; or in the controversies— perhaps leading to firing or transfer—over clergy who have the tactlessness to preach the painful prophetic word in its contemporary relevance or to dwell too vividly on the disturbing demands of *agape*. The "pillars of society" who support the churches and synagogues tend to be firmly based in the modern world. It is no exaggeration to conclude that the institutions of religion have been largely captured by modern consciousness.

But is there, nevertheless, some special leverage that the churches and synagogues may possess? If the "salt of the earth" are mainly savorless, is there still some catalyst that may return them to spicy sharpness? The answer rests in the latent power of mythic imagery to reclaim response. At least adherents of organized religion regularly expose themselves to the once-potent archetypes of value and meaning that define their respective faiths. If the myths come alive with power for the transformation of consciousness, there is hope for renewal within the traditional faiths. That is, in the language of theistic mythology, if God wills to revive his people, and, through them, to redeem his world, he can surely do so, despite all obstacles. Still in this language we may say: it is the irresistible and mysterious power of God that holds the final answer to the problems of resavoring the salt and renewing human consciousness for abundant life in the post-modern world.

In sum, then, our need is for a miracle. If the institutional religions of our world are to offer us much ground for hope, something will have to happen within them that we can neither predict nor control. This does not mean that we should abandon hope; on the contrary, the power of the great biblical images to renew response has been proven powerfully in the past, time and again. We have no ground for the despairing supposition that this power has been exhausted for all the future. Even dead myths have a strange capacity for resurrection. But we also have no ground for the (basically technolatrous) dream of manipulating the consciousness of the coming age through the leverage of institutional religion. "Thy Kingdom come!" may be breathed as a prayer; it must not be interpreted as an imperative ordering up spiritual reforms on demand. Our age is surely in need of a miracle. God only knows if we shall receive one through his earthly followers.

POSTSCRIPT FOR JEWS AND CHRISTIANS

I have perhaps written too distantly, about "them," in the foregoing. This chapter was written primarily for *you,* leadership and laity alike, to draw your attention to the possibilities for fresh emphasis and renewal within our great biblical faiths. It is through *your* eyes that the new vision must be seen; it is through *your* minds that the implications of post-modern belief must be sorted out; it is through *your* hearts that the warmth of new holism, homeostasis and creativity must be felt—if God's miracle is to come through Christianity and Judaism in our time.

Institutions are cumbersome and slow; but they can be moved by the mysterious power of a few persons fired with a contagious truth. If you are persuaded that your faith has a providential role to play in the transition to a new organismic age in human history, speak to others of your convictions and live them—joyfully—in the sight of your neighbors and before your God. *Your* responsiveness will be the measure of our common hope.

8. HOPE IN EDUCATIONAL INSTITUTIONS

At the start of the previous chapter I touched briefly on institutional education as offering hope for the regrounding of society in a transformed consciousness that would be appropriate to a livable post-modern world. I reported that in many of my eager students' eyes, such education seems an insufferably slow and elitist path to the nurturing of the urgently needed organic values of the new age. Compared to a media "blitz" or mass conversion through some miracle, the leisurely pace of institutional education does seem snaillike and cerebral; but a media campaign, as we saw, is improbable and inappropriate, and miracles are unpredictable and uncontrollable. Consequently it may be time for a closer look at education.

As a professional educator myself, I am spared some of the illusions of omnipotence that some outside the field seem to nurture on our behalf. But I have from firsthand experience learned to respect the power of education to touch and transform persons. Furthermore, in the developed nations of the modern world education at substantial levels is nearly universal, and in the United States even post-secondary education is becoming the normal expectation of vast numbers rather than the privilege of a narrow few. It is not wise, therefore, to dismiss education as effete or elitist. Slow the process may be, as compared to other imagined means of change and, indeed, as compared to the historic need; but the very rhythms of education themselves, as unhurriable as the rhythms of the seasons and as subtle as the ripening of fruit, may contribute a permanence and stability to the metamorphoses they bring about that helps to reconcile us to the time they take.

Assuming, then, that schools will remain important institutional vehicles for education, for better or for worse, in the foreseeable future (despite Ivan Illich's ardent plea, with which I have much sympathy, for "deschooling" society),* let us take a look at the possible applications of Polymythic Organicism to institutional education. Education to remake society will itself first have to be remade in significant ways. What are some of the basic goals that future educators should seek?

I

One major value suggested by Polymythic Organicism is, as we have seen, the cultivation of holistic mutuality among well-differentiated parts. A pervasive disposition in this direction within institutional education at all levels would reinforce some efforts that are currently already being made and might suggest some further ways in which they could be extended.

Primary education, almost universal in the modern world, is an important area for the laying of adequate foundations. These foundations affect the whole person, and through whole persons the whole society. Fundamental holism

*Ivan Illich, *Deschooling Society* (N.Y.: Harper & Row, 1970).

expressed and learned in early years through challenges to cognitive growth, avenues of social interaction, and intuitions of feeling and perceiving, would help to counteract the pressures toward reduction, fragmentation, and alienation which we have seen to be so harmful within the common consciousness of the modern world.

In subject matter, first, primary education rooted in holistic values should deal in a rhythmic way both with parts and with their interconnections within greater and lesser unities. The primary emphasis should be on some whole, letting the patterns of the "big picture" take shape first, and allowing the details of the parts to emerge out of initial vagueness, as a photographic print emerges gradually into greater and greater sharpness in the developing tray. At one extreme, consciousness of the global earth, as one shared domain of mankind and nature, enfolded in a single sphere without edges, might well precede any great emphasis on nations or states or even local governments. On the other hand, the child's own person—body, belief, feelings, and family—might constitute the holistic microcosm for intensely interesting study. Sometimes, equally well, the emphasis might be intermediate, for example on the concreteness of the local fire station in contrast to the abstraction of "municipal government." Organicism values the distinctness of well-differentiated particulars as well as the mutual functioning of wholes in which such parts function. Thus the fire station as well-differentiated functioning unit is worth close attention in its own right. In its own right, however, it is a whole, within which well-differentiated subparts function in an instructive analogy to the way in which it functions as a part of a larger whole. Holistic educational interest, therefore, will shift rhythmically from looking at the fire station as a part of something larger, to which it contributes its distinctive functions, and as a whole in itself, made up of parts which function variously to make possible the larger social intention we summarize as "fire fighting" that gives them context, meaning, and unity. The subparts of the fire station, though, are also made up out of sub-subparts. The fire engine, for example, may first and more importantly be a functioning whole which has a use within the unifying intention of the fire station, but it also can be seen as giving unifying intention to the carburator, the transmission, the pumps, and so on, that it, as a subpart, integrates with functional meaning. True; and such sub-subparts as pumps and carburators themselves are meaningful societies of parts (valves and jets and gaskets, etc.) which they unify with their own particular functional intention in the larger unity of the fire truck, which itself is a unity of functional intention in the larger unity of the fire station, which itself is a unity of functional intention in the larger unity of municipal government, which itself is a unity of functional intention . . . in more complex societies of societies of societies. The rhythms of holistic interest swing back and forth over the whole range of subject matter, from self to cosmos, but always with emphasis on the significant wholes of which our meaningful world is made.

The tools for learning, too—the language skills (reading and writing) and the concepts of quantity and precision in abstraction (mathematics)—should show holistic rhythms between the differentiated particular and the primary unifying context. The *word* is a significant whole prior to the letters that spell it. Similarly, the *sentence* in which the word is used is logically prior to its words and is, as it were, the functional justification for their use. But the sentence, though a functional unity at one level of use, is only a part of the *story* which called for it. The functional intention imparted to the story by the teller is the prior whole that gives meaningful point to all the sentences needed to tell it. So the primacy goes to storytellers and to stories, not to letters, though letters are interesting in their own right for what they can do and not do, and for how they may go together in the service of meaningful discourse.

Likewise numbers are interesting only for their significant

relations to one another, and those relations are mainly interesting within the context of still more relations. In higher mathematics those relations would all be abstract, but in the primary years the relevant relations involve the more concrete contexts of application: the exciting discovery of the quantifiability of the world around, its hospitality to the same simple set of abstractions we call numbers, and the charming exactness and dependability of the connections among these wonderful concepts that follow their own rules so neatly.

The curricular approach both to subject matter and to the basic tools for learning will be affected by the rhythms of holistic values in primary education, then; in like manner the social ambience of the classroom as it involves both students and teachers must be touched as well. In the class, the principle of mutuality among well-differentiated parts should foster delight in the differences between the children—in race or religion or experience—at the same time that such differences are transcended in a sensed community based on common interest and intention. Children need to have a chance to learn and celebrate their own uniqueness and the distinctiveness of other peers; simultaneously they need an opportunity to learn and practice the skills, habits, and feelings of mutual accommodation in the interest of a unifying purpose. In a holistic primary education, further, there would be a proper context for dealing with the inevitable differences between teacher and child. There would be no need to find such differences embarrassing; there is no use in pretending that the teacher is not older and more experienced than his or her pupils, and in a position of leadership, protection, and authority. A healthy organism illustrates mutuality among its suborgans, but there is subordination as well. The teacher in a holistic primary classroom will not be merely a dispenser of information. The teacher-facilitator will constantly be listening and responsive to the pupils of the class, but the class's collective intention needs to be focused, refined, and creatively directed by a single center of purpose.

Shot through the cognitive-curricular and social-interactive, and inseparable from them, is the affective-perceptual side of primary education. Children suited for a livable post-modern world need to learn to feel and see themselves and their world holistically. There are endless opportunities in primary education for developing sensibilities in looking and listening, touching and feeling. Children would be helped to see the landscape as a living whole, the birds and the butterflies in the network of constant interactive relationships that binds themselves and all life together. In music, the harmonies of tones and interactions of rhythms would be listened to before the individual parts; in art, the unity of the painting or the intention of the photographer or the overall meaning of the sculpture would be stressed before—and only later related to —technique. In these ways, and many more as general strategies of education are worked out into particular tactics by creative teachers, the values of holism need to permeate primary education and through it encourage needed forms of consciousness.

II

Secondary education allows opportunities for further expression of holistic values. I have worked extensively as a consultant to high schools and have been encouraged at how much interest I have found in creating new forms that can embody such values.

At the curricular level, first, a properly holistic secondary education must retain and intensify the rhythms between meaningful parts and larger wholes. That means, specifically, that the high school experience should be a judicious mix between disciplinary and integrative efforts in each grade. The disciplines of specific methods and areas of knowledge are important to retain; this is true not merely, though partly, because multi- and interdisciplinary educational efforts are futile without the disciplines to draw upon and integrate. It is also vital to retain the specific disciplines because they are—or ought to be—interesting and meaningful in their own right. Each discipline, history, English, the various sciences (or the like), is properly conceived as a significant whole with its own unifying intention, though of course always related to the other disciplines through the larger unifying intention that constitutes the educational program as a whole. Each deserves an opportunity for single-minded attention. It will be important for the citizens of the post-modern world to be able to think historically—to know how to relate to the past, to have a sense of the larger time-frames of historical thought, to be familiar with the methods of weighing the adequacy of historical judgments. It will be important, similarly, to have a population well grounded in the use and appreciation of language—all should have the mastery of basic skills in verbal expression both for the obvious utility of such mastery and for its intrinsic satisfactions. It will be important, again, for men and women to understand the sciences, both to learn what fascinating things the sciences tell us about the world we live in and to gain a proper sense of the difference between science as a secular human enterprise and scientism as a worldview, a metaphysic, the mythic matrix of a religious phenomenon that the post-modern world must learn to outgrow.

Holistic secondary education must recognize the meaningful integrity of the various disciplines, then, but the rhythms of holistic interest should not stop with that. Throughout the high school years there ought to be constant opportunity to relate the disciplines, to see them as intelligible parts and subparts of larger wholes variously approached. The individual disciplines must not be allowed (as too often happens at present) to become isolated structures without ties to one another or, even worse, to become politicized into departmental power blocs locked in endless rivalry and mutual denigration. Instead, the educational intention as a unity of purpose must be acknowledged as dominant, and the individual disciplines, while recognized and respected, then be seen as organic parts mutually related to this higher whole. Rather than "building" a curriculum by putting separate disciplinary blocks together as though these had primary and individual existence, holistic educators will need to seek various modes of differentiating their central aim: facilitating understanding of the world for fruitful life in it. This inverts the entire typical approach. The disciplines, on this new approach, are seen as *among* the ways of differentiating the larger intention of secondary education, not as the *only* (or even primary) ways. Just as the story takes precedence over the particular sentences that serve to tell it; just as the unifying intention of the fire department is prior to any of the equipment, however vital, that is used to express that intention; so pride of place in post-modern educational efforts will go to the larger unifying aims of education.

"Interdisciplinary" courses may be ill-named, then, on this understanding of the priorities in learning. The typical reductionistic thought patterns of modern consciousness suggests that the parts (the disciplines) are primary and that any efforts called interdisciplinary would be mechanical derivatives of merely putting certain disciplines together. In fact, if the holistic viewpoint is adopted, the larger or differently designed unities are no less fundamental—perhaps even more basic—ways of letting the educational endeavor become differentiated. We might more properly speak of "integrative" courses, then, in order to get away from language that suggests a misleading educational model.

The opportunities for integrative courses at the secondary level are literally beyond counting. I have been involved in helping to plan a great variety in the last few years through the constructive efforts of the National Humanities Faculty, an organization founded to bring together interested high school teachers and administrators with university consultants in just such efforts. Some of the integrative courses I have seen have chosen to approach a cross section of the world through broad topics, like the Concept of Success (in religion, in science, in literature or film), or Revolutions and Counterrevolutions (in art, science, morality, as well as history and government); some have chosen to expand outward through overlapping contexts of greater generality, as in Self, Society, Nature, and Supernature; some have chosen to focus on a particular place (usually one's own city) and see it freshly and thoroughly from its geological history through its social interactions, government, economic problems, courting practices, artistic expressions, religious life, connections to the larger world around, to its ecological problems or possibilities and its possible futures; some have concentrated on a historical period or have compared major periods; some have selected two or three or four cities for careful scrutiny and have concluded with the imaginary design (including architecture, government, social mores, economic system, etc.) of their own ideal city; some have attempted to integrate understanding of current events, as in Technology and Modern Values or in Environment and Culture (dealing carefully with substantive scientific principles involved as well as with social, historical, political, religious, ethical issues through field trips, literature, laboratory, and interview)—all have required intellectual rigor (discipline) but are not "disciplinary" or even, in the old sense, inter- or multidisciplinary. They have been integrative from within the larger intention of secondary education and, though hampered by occasional misunderstanding from modern reductionist consciousness and frequent obstacles from modern departmentally dominated structures of high school organization, they represent in my experience the promising green shoots that suggest what may yet develop within a more organismically cultivated curriculum needed to nourish a post-modern world.

The social and affective aspects of secondary education, briefly, must be designed to follow suit. I have found, for instance, that integrative courses are impossible to teach successfully in the typical social form of one-teacher-in-front-of-a-class. They are essentially different from traditional disciplinary courses, in which this traditional social form appropriately grew up. Integrative courses in principle require a team of teachers, not only for the sake of the different contributions that they may make from their different disciplinary backgrounds, but also (and even more importantly) for the sake of the interaction that occurs within the planning sessions and in the actual teaching. The teaching team (even if it be only two persons) is a community of peers, and the mutuality within differentiation that must emerge from the successful teaching together of an integrative course is one of the important fruits of holistic education. Furthermore, the students themselves, observing the reality of teacher mutuality within functioning differentiated unity, learn to perceive their own relationships to the faculty and to each other in fresh, holistic ways. Peer teaching then becomes more natural and more effective: students start sharing with each other in ways that their growing maturity makes possible and in ways that the format of integrated education makes easy. The whole feeling toward the educational enterprise thus gradually changes. It is not something that is done *to* the students, but something that the students and the faculty are doing together —something in which individual differences are not embarrassments but assets.

Ideally, integrative education should involve all types of students, certainly not only those who are planning to continue their academic work beyond the secondary level. Those who do not excel in verbal skills will still have much to contribute in a properly holistic high school. I have seen creative ways in which students who have learned to think of themselves as academic "losers" have been the focus of efforts to draw them back to the educational enterprise through integrative courses in which their skills and interests—in automobile maintenance, in community activities, in their personal situations and local contexts—have been harnessed meaningfully.

The values of holism, then, aim at transforming the high

schools into centers of fresh possibility for genuine learning and fruitful mutuality: richness and wholeness cognitively, socially, and emotionally for the coming age. That aim, of course, will not be easily achieved. Let no one be deluded about the obstacles posed by entrenched attitudes and practices. Merely wishing for holism will not make our educational system whole. A great goal sometimes painfully measures the length of the journey ahead; but without great goals we merely drift. Transforming secondary education by holistic values will require intense struggle, but will be worth the effort. It will be part of the struggle for the soul of the post-modern world.

III

College education is an opportunity for the embodiment of holistic values at a yet more thoroughgoing level. The dialectic between the traditional disciplines and the integrative differentiations of the educational intention should begin, this time, with the integrative. Assuming that the high schools have provided the student with adequate disciplinary foundations, the college experience can begin with the excitement of a fresh start. Perhaps this might be accomplished by abandoning the entire "course" approach to education: different hurdles to be leaped one by one as the student runs the academic race. Instead, the student might be offered a year or two with a tutor-adviser in which to define his or her interests and, within broadly defined areas essential to the educational aim, in which to qualify for concentrated upper-level work appropriate both to academic rigor and to self-definition.

The general areas within which each student might be required to demonstrate competence by the end of the first phase of college education would include: first, the area of conceptual clarity, involving languages of all sorts from English and German to FORTRAN and mathematics, and including conceptual skills such as logic and rhetoric; second, the area of factual content, drawing on the various sciences, both

physical and social, and emphasizing the methods of discovery
—the process as well as the product—of the factual disciplines
in a rapidly changing cognitive world; third, the area of value
assessment, focusing on literature and the fine arts and music
and drama as opportunities for the enlargement of valuational
experience and the sharpening of value intuitions; and, finally,
the area of comprehensive reflection, including the
omnirelevant concerns of philosophy, history, and religion.
These areas, rather than departments, might be seen as the
natural units of differentiation in the early phase of the college
experience. Courses of lectures or packages of self-instructional
material might be made available, richly, from the resources of
the college, but none of this would be required for those who
could demonstrate competence in pertinent areas without it.
The tutor-adviser and the student would discuss the tactics to
be followed and would adjust directions as opportunities,
needs, and developing self-discovery might dictate. In some
such way, including group discussions among tutees and
out-of-school contacts between advisers and advisees, the
image and reality of education would be shifted significantly in
the early college years: away from the assumption that gaining
an education is tantamount to taking a number of courses, and
toward the realization that becoming educated is an active
process in which the institution serves as resource and
encouragement for the differentiation and enrichment of the
individual learner within a context of educational intentions
toward wholeness and integrity.

The romance of these first years of the collegiate experience
should whet the maturing student's appetite for the rigors of
further, deeper exploration within one or more specific
discipline. Once qualified to enter upper-level work, the
student would plunge into a major field designed to probe
deeply into particularities, the relevance of which to wider
educational contexts has already been perceived. These
encounters with the rigors of higher education might, but need
not exclusively be, defined in terms of the traditional

disciplines. If so, they would be seen as significant differentiations within the larger educational enterprise and openly chosen as such. If not, they might be designed around some specific problem area: the protection of the natural environment, the establishment of social justice for minority groups, the prevention of international conflict, the adjustment of society to alternative energy sources, or the like. Either way, the hard work of intellectual precision would be required—and visibly justified by the needs of the chosen major field itself within the larger educational intention.

Finally, after the phases of romance and of rigor, the college experience should be climaxed by the reunion of romance and rigor in an upper-level integrative multidisciplinary experience that allows the sharing of individual expertise with other advanced students from various fields. In a culminating seminar or project that draws together people who have gone separate ways during the upper-level phase, some use should be made of the rigors of the major field in a larger context again. Each student would need to assume the role of expositor for his or her particular field, explaining and applying it responsibly, without violating its rigors while making its contributions make sense to the other intelligent nonexperts in the group. Since teaching a subject is the best possible method of really learning it, this climactic integrative experience should reap multiple dividends in holistic college education.

IV

Postgraduate and professional education is currently the most specialized and least in keeping with holistic values of any of the levels in education. The economic pressures and the disintegrative, overtechnical values of modern consciousness are here nearest to the surface, just as students here are nearest to their specialized professional roles in modern society. But there is nothing intrinsic to graduate education that forbids its transformation, if there is a will to do so, into more inclusive, contextual, and mutual forms. Already some medical schools around the United States, in Florida, Pennsylvania, and elsewhere, have taken bold steps to broaden the education of future medical doctors by adding pertinent courses in the humanities and social sciences. Medical ethics, for example, is and ought to be a major concern of the medical profession; holistic educational theory would applaud and enlarge such pioneering movements. Similarly, schools of law have begun to open themselves to the careful study of the larger context within which lawyers operate. Schools of engineering, too, are becoming alert to the need for introducing the reflective disciplines into their typically tight and demanding curricula. My own experience participating in a team-taught course in ethics at one of the engineering schools at Purdue University has reinforced my conviction both as to the need and as to the potential enthusiasm for such curricular opportunities when holistic values are put into general practice. If introduced properly, these changes will not need to diminish the appropriate rigor of graduate and professional training; they will instead add a needed rhythm between such necessary rigors and the equally necessary contexts of relevance to the professions.

I have addressed these first remarks to the needs of professional training for holistic reform, but they are no less pertinent to the academic graduate schools or departments that turn out the scholars and teachers of our colleges and universities. The academic, discipline-oriented departments are typically no less corrupted by the hyperspecialized, professional values than are the professional schools themselves. Even the field of philosophy itself, where holism should be first of all expected if philosophy is held true to its comprehensive interest in all contexts, has largely succumbed to modern professionalization and tubular vision. If post-modern educational institutions are truly to offer hope for a healthier consciousness, the education of the educators will itself be in for some deep reforms. Whether these reforms will rise gradually from below, as new generations of graduate professors take the reins in graduate departments and in teachers' colleges here and there, or whether they will come suddenly, due to student pressures or mass "conversion," I shall not speculate. It may not come at all, of course; or it may not come in time to help in the transformation of society in needed ways. But the need and the possibilities are there. This book is in part an appeal that they be recognized in time to help us make a humane transition into the post-modern world.

Finally, but not least important, I wish to add a word about the vital need for vastly more emphasis on continuing, or adult, education for the living of our transition. We all, not just the young, face jolting times of unfamiliar challenges; the educational institutions must, on holistic principles, draw the mature and the elderly into the community of those attempting to understand these challenges and trying to respond to them with creativity and dignity. Perhaps as never in history, a major civilization is in need of reeducating a whole population both in fresh understanding of fact and in new values for a new day. "Without vision the people perish." The schools and colleges are meant to be society's organs of vision. We all need to go back to school. I know how much I need it. I know, also, how many high school teachers in midcareer feel the need of it. And I believe that all—farmers and accountants and auto mechanics alike—should have the opportunity to discover their own need, and fulfill it. Some might particularly need to understand the historic forces that are operating on our society so as to live with a greater sense of context; others might wish to learn nonpolluting and socially beneficial skills or avenues of expression so as to live with a heightened sense of community. Society at large would be the beneficiary; a holistic society would joyfully make major (defense-budget sized) resources available to all its people to take advantage of the educational opportunities that exist or might be developed. The post-modern world, if it is to be a humane and livable one, needs to be an age of education nourished by the values of organismic holism.

The identification of a need, of course, is no guarantee that the need will be met. No one can consider such great social transformations without realizing how utopian they sound, given the realities of our time. A miracle, in education no less than in religion (as we saw in chapter 6), seems called for. But clarity requires that we not allow the fog of dismay over present prospects to obscure our vision of what the real needs are. A necessary condition for great revolutions is the capacity to dream great dreams. When large dreams galvanize large energies, new realities rise from the rubble of old impossibilities.

V

The other two values which characterize the basic profile of Polymythic Organicism are inner self-limitation, or homeostasis, and creativity. I shall treat them together in this final section, not because there is less to say about each in its applicability to education—whole chapters and books deserve to be written—but, rather, to illustrate the important dialectical linkage between them. They are, after all, the values of Apollo and Dionysus, the Greek gods of order and divine frenzy, respectively. Apollo is the patron of self-restraint; the symmetrical, the restrained, the cool, the lucid. "Nothing in excess" is the Apollonian creed. Dionysus, on the other hand, stands for the bursting of barriers, the infinite potential for novelty, transcendence, ecstasy. Dionysus presides over revelry, frolic, intoxication; Apollo stands aloof and cool, always in control.

The Greeks knew that both of these basic value-sets are literally vital. Without Apollonian restraint, life tears itself to pieces in the anarchy of runaway wildness; but without Dionysian zest, life withers and congeals. Self-restraint is essential for health in body and mind, and so also, on the other hand, is the sparkle of novelty and the lure of risk-laden transcendence. The two gods were consequently intertwined in Greek consciousness. Ironically, the primary temple of lucid Apollo, at Delphi, was presided over by a most unlucid priestess in a dark cavern who intoned obscure oracular sayings in the name of the patron of lofty intelligibility! Even the temple precincts themselves were abandoned regularly, for a season, to the priests and followers of Dionysus. The two gods seemed to be recognized as opposite sides of the same fundamental intuition into basic values, different faces of equally deep needs. Not only the frenzy of revelry, but also those marvelously ordered and symmetrical Greek dramas so admired by Apollonian literature professors (as well as by audiences) were in the domain of Dionysus. The ancient Greeks knew better than to let these gods become too far separated from one another. They kept them in constant dialectical contact.

In the same way, then, organismic education for the post-modern world will need to balance Apollonian homeostasis with Dionysian creativity. It will be essential to learn limits, and how to live responsibly with them, at every stage in the educational process; and, at the same time, it will be vital that acknowledgement of limits not be the death of creative exuberance.

Primary education ought to manifest this balance both in the curriculum and in the general life of the school. Children need to learn to come to terms with their own finitude and to learn ways of developing attitudes and responses appropriate to the constraints of human life. They are, for example, during the primary school years becoming aware of death—it may claim a relative, a pet—and it is for many a profound and disturbing discovery. Yet there are very few places in current primary curricula for thoughtful, sustained teaching about the subject. It would be a fascinating and helpful area for study. It could lead into, or develop out of, examination of the ecological cycles of food-chain and decomposition. It could reinforce the sense of holistic unity with the universe of life. But, at the same time, it should be linked with the study of life's creativity, the inventiveness of life-forms which manage to adapt to the most amazing conditions, the joyful affirmation of existence that is symbolized by birth and growth in every species.

To take another example, primary level history need not drop its tendency to celebrate the triumphs and successes of the heroes of the past. But in addition, balancing the picture should be the record, as well, of the frustration that attends all great enterprises, the loss of achieved heights, the missing of opportunities. It should not come as a later surprise that even heroes make mistakes and lose nearly as often as they win— and are still heroes, for all that. The celebration of victory is itself flat without the three-dimensional sense of the constant possibility of defeat. Both are needed. Both are real. A properly organismic primary curriculum will not shrink from presenting both the wine of glory and the taste of ashes.

Similarly, the personal experience of each primary student should reflect the dialogue of Dionysus and Apollo. The zest of playful learning, the wonder of felt growth in developing capacities, the heady sense of achievement are the substance and reward of education that is rooted properly in the living powers of healthy children. These are the gifts of Dionysus. But the treasures of Apollo are essential, too. They consist in the conceptual ability to distinguish and clarify, and in the emotional control that makes possible the mutuality in community that is the basis of holistic education.

Secondary education, college, and graduate training all have need of the same dialectic between the values of homeostasis and creativity. As knowledge of the world becomes more refined, more detailed exploration is appropriate on the limits and the possibilities surrounding us. We need to know the facts. Only in the context of full cognitive grasp will our policies and attitudes be in touch with reality. Secondary and postsecondary curricula will need to incorporate continual opportunities to stay abreast of the best information available on the boundary conditions within which post-modern society will need to live. There should never again be the general naïvete over natural limits that has led, in the United States, to confusion and skepticism over the genuiness, say, of the long-term energy crisis that confronts our petroleum-addicted lifestyle. Education to reality has an obligation to maintain public awareness of the limits within which self-controlled styles of life are essential for survival with dignity and morality.

On the other hand, the efforts of education at the higher levels, like the lower, need not all be Apollonian. The flutes of Dionysus need to sound as well, and the institutions of learning are capable of responding to the call. The treasures of new possibilities for fulfillment in human life are available. The joys of great literature, the challenges of philosophy, the ecstasies of dance and music—ways of growing in quality of life without exceeding the material limits of the finite earth or oppressing the neighbor—are available in abundance. These treasures represent the inventiveness and creativity of benign growth. They should not be overlooked by students or teachers as vital parts of the normal educational experience; neither should they be withheld from the average inhabitants of the future world, whatever their position, age, or aptitude. Arts and crafts, poetry and dance, philosophy and history and painting, should flourish as never before in history within a society that transfers its creative energy from the making and selling of material goods to the satisfactions available through the Dionysian gifts of universally available higher education.

It is a lovely vision. Perhaps it is possible. The educational institutions exist, if our society has the will to use them. But much would need to change, both within institutional education itself and within society at large before these health-giving dreams could become reality. I have attempted to suggest some of the changes within education that would give us grounds for hope from that direction. I am not making predictions; I am pointing directions. The heavy weight of precedent and power is opposed to the realization of these hopes. But the powers of the modern world are reaching the point, as we have seen, of self-nullification; and the precedents of the past are of dubious authority for our time of transition. Society at large must change, of course; but society at large *is* changing. Our challenge is to influence these changes in needed directions. Let us therefore conclude with a look, from this perspective, at our changing society—particularly at the economic and political institutions that represent the current powers that be—to see what hoped-for changes in them might conspire, with religion and education, to lead us into a livable post-modern world.

9. HOPE IN ECONOMICS AND POLITICS

By the time we have reached economics and politics, on our figurative modern aircraft, we have reached the real engines that power us through history. The same may not be true in all societies; religion or race or other springs of motivation may at some times and in some places constitute overriding interests; it is an ethnocentric mistake for Marxists to generalize from their own modern consciousness to all other cultures and eras, concerning the so-called "material" basis for all significant historical processes. But in the modern world of scientific technology and high industrialization, wherever it has spread—east from Europe to the Soviet Union and Japan, and west to the United States and Canada—the Marxist vision has much point. The main propulsive forces in *our* civilization, the principal motivators in *our* typical consciousness, the true functioning religion-surrogates underlying *our* dominant ideologies (ironically, both capitalist and Marxist versions), are economic and political.

That may not always be the case in the future, of course,

since it is not an iron law of human life that wealth and power must dominate all other interests. Indeed, we are rapidly learning that the unchecked pursuit of wealth and power has led our modern world to the edge of disaster, and that post-modern consciousness will need to have a different center —one that keeps the interests of economics and politics in better balance with the rest of those values that make life worth living.

Still, we must get where we are going from where we are. Passage through the difficult transition will continue to be propelled in large measure by the engines of economic and political institutions. The purpose of this last chapter is to reflect on those institutions from the viewpoint of Polymythic Organicism. What are the critical issues in economics and politics when examined in terms of homeostasis, holism, and creativity? Where ought we to look for reforms that will make the deepest difference? What changes would bring the greatest hope? Beyond looking and hoping, what might we do personally to make our hopes more likely to be realized?

I

The organic principle of internal stability and restraint, what I have here called homeostasis, points up areas of critically needed reform in both political and economic domains. And it highlights as historically significant some of the thinking and working that is currently going on around us.

One of the obvious morals of modern times is that the pursuit and exercise of political power needs to be placed within effective internal constraints. This is not a new realization. But in the twentieth century, with Hitler and Stalin as horrible examples of the consequences of unchecked power, greater sensitivity than ever to the need for political restraints should have been expected. Oddly enough, the United States in midcentury, however, came close to dulling its awareness of this need beyond the point of no return. Perhaps the fatigue of war, the anxiety of sudden emergence into a superpower stalemate with the Soviet Union, and the hubris of self-declared world leadership (and policing), numbed the nation to its growing danger. The uncovering of the great Nixonian conspiracy in the 1970s, however, and the aftershocks from continuing disclosures of well-advanced totalitarian practices—the "invisible government" of a vast undercover intelligence apparatus—thriving under the pretense of democracy and the protection of official secrecy, have resensitized many in this country to the pressing values of political restraints.

From the perspective of Polymythic Organicism, then, in line with its concern for homeostatic controls, the efforts that are being made to institutionalize and extend the political protections of disclosure, due process, and division of power are significant historically as hope-bearing reforms for our times of transition.

Secrecy in government at every level is a potential threat to the values of political restraint. What is not known does not need to be accounted for. When no response is demanded, responsibility dies. Therefore disclosure is one of the essential dimensions of political reform in our time. And there are some grounds for hope on this dimension. In the United States the "people's lobby," Common Cause, has used popular revulsion against the Nixon scandals skillfully to support "sunshine" laws in Congress where, despite natural political reluctance, major steps have been taken to open government records and even to disclose the financial interests of politicians themselves to public scrutiny. Common Cause has also worked successfully for disclosure through the courts, and was of significant assistance in this regard to the investigation of the Watergate scandals themselves. Other interests and efforts are also on the side of increased disclosure of the uses of power.

Congressional investigations sometimes do much good. The Senate Select ("Watergate") Committee alerted the nation to its peril. The modern media, likewise, are instruments in the service of the needs of our transition. They may be unwitting in this role, but they are strong. Their "message" may be the modern culture that we must learn to leave behind, but as potent allies in support of disclosure and responsibility in government they are to be welcomed and respected. At the same time, all the disclosure in the world will be of no value without active citizen response to what is revealed. Post-modern society must develop potent structures of public interest to counterbalance the special interests that now infiltrate decision-making processes at every level. Disclosure must not mean merely the lowering of all barriers protecting politicians from the pressures of lobbyists for the various economic blocs; to prevent this will require an alert public effectively organized to use its information wisely.

Due process, second, is the internal restraint that comes from the accountability of political power to a system of laws. It is a primary check on the arbitrary and capricious exercise of raw ability to impose one's will on others. Seen from the standpoint of respect for homeostatic restraint, those who are working to extend the protections of civil liberties are fulfilling a historic mission not only to honor the intentions of the founders of the American Constitution but also to assist at the birth of the post-modern world. There are powerful obstacles confronting such efforts, of course. The mood of the Nixon Supreme Court is less responsive to appeals for civil protection than was its predecessor, and the effects of this change will be felt not only for many years to come but also everywhere within the judicial system of the United States. But there is hope, still, in the persistent efforts of the American Civil Liberties Union and allied groups as they work not only through the courts, reminding them that justices, no less than others wielding power, must recognize their duty to uphold justice, but also with legislators in the preparation of laws that will strengthen the restraints placed upon the use of power. The battle is hard but not hopeless. And it is historic: much of the quality of the post-modern world will depend upon its outcome.

Division of power, third, is a means of restraining the ruthless drive towards maximizing political strength by institutionalizing friction-surfaces and countervailing forces within the political structures themselves. It is an old principle, one that was incorporated within the American Constitution by its framers—and one incorporated largely out of bitter suspicion that the tendency of unchecked political rule is to sour into tyranny. Again, the value of political homeostasis would urge support for efforts that preserve dynamic tensions among the holders of power. To continue reference to the United States government, the imbalance of recent years in favor of the presidency at the expense of the Congress and the courts has been contributory to the dangers of presidential corruption and, in principle, to the not-so-unthinkable dangers of presidential dictatorship. We should now be aware of the vital interest a healthy organismic society has in the maintenance of balance where balance is due. The hubris of the Nixon presidency ended in the nemesis of a Court and Congress united against the excesses of executive power. It is important that Americans learn from their traumatic experience that political imbalances are dangerous. Congressional or judicial tyranny would be equally undesirable; the "strong" presidencies, after all, arose in reaction to congressional excesses as well as to the emergency conditions of depression and war. Homeostatic balance needs constant readjustment if health is to be maintained without painful chills and fevers. Fortunately, there are strong movements afoot supporting these values. The interests of the various organs of national government and the interests of the civil service—which remains somewhat independent of capricious or dictatorial political behavior thanks, ironically, to its own bureaucratic inertia—work in behalf of historically desirable outcomes. And, no less ironically, conservative pressures to enhance local political power may also be unwittingly in defense of the limitations of central authority that must be a feature of a balanced organismic post-modern political structure. Such movements may not be strong enough, of course, to resist the tendency for power to centralize and expand. But those with homeostatic values will work to reinforce their efforts.

Not only political but also economic giantism and overcentralization have to be reformed and reversed in our transition time. The unbalancing effects of hugeness on human life is incalculable but deep. The enormous corporations, national and international, develop a momentum out of scale with other needs and interests; the system of interlocking economic giants squeezes out alternative styles of life and forces on the whole of modern society what Ivan Illich calls a "radical monopoly"[1] of goods and services. The automotive giants, to take but one example, are in Illich's sense radical monopolists.

> Cars can thus monopolize traffic. They can shape a city into their image—practically ruling out locomotion on foot or by bicycle in Los Angeles. . . . That motor traffic curtails the right to walk, not that more people drive Chevies than Fords, constitutes radical monopoly.[2]

Another, poignant, example of the radical monopolizing effects of modern industrial technique in the service of economic efficiency through standardization is found in the experience of the Shakers, a religious community of craftsmen and craftswomen which flourished (despite its insistence on recruiting by conversion rather than procreation) before the development of mass production. The Shakers are still famous for the quality of their handcrafted furniture and other simple but ingenious designs, but their healthy economic base was undercut by competition from economic scale. The Shakers, considering their workmanship and style of production to be a part of their religious commitment, refused to cut corners on quality or to join the mass-production monopoly; and they paid the supreme price for their faithfulness by dying out as a community rather than compromise. In this way, the modern economic system drove a whole style of life, a religion, and a craft tradition out of existence and insured the increasing homogenization of modern society.

> Radical monopoly exists where a major tool [such as mass production technique] rules out natural competence. Radical monopoly imposes compulsory consumption and thereby restricts personal autonomy. It constitutes a special kind of social control because it is enforced by means of the imposed consumption of a standard product that only large institutions can provide.[3]

Henri Bergson once joked that he didn't care how standardized, through mass production, his hats might become as long as he could furnish the interior of his head as he pleased. The joke, alas, seems to have been turned on the modern world: we have found that the requirements of the economic system force us all to conform, and the interiors of our heads—our preferences, tastes, and beliefs—are not to be spared, either, once radical economic monopolies take full effect.

The answer to economic giantism is decentralization and scaling down, to human levels, the forces of production and distribution. E. F. Schumacher has been spreading the gospel of economic smallness[4] not only in writings and speeches but also in practice through his London-based Intermediate Technology Development Group, which assists developing nations (primarily) in the invention and application of appropriate technologies to suit their needs without falling prey to the radical monopolies that the modern world assumes they must have. Schumacher's work is highly encouraging from the point of view of the organismic value of homeostatic restraint, since he is showing that there is a strong market for technological solutions that are not dependent upon more and more so-called "economies of scale" and constantly increasing profligate expenditures of energy resources. The techniques that Schumacher offers to his clients tend to be simple, cheap, and local. When applied, they have the sophistication of obviousness—the highest form of invention. A brick-making unit; an egg-carton machine; a plow drawn by a cable and winch rather than a heavy, petroleum-hungry tractor—these are the sorts of technologies that Schumacher provides. Taken together, they are an alternative to the gigantic economic machine that we normally take for granted as fated. Schumacher, with a few like him, is challenging the worldwide radical monopoly of modern megaeconomics.

Not only in the developing nations but also in our overdeveloped ones, this challenge is being made to economic assumptions on size and centralization. It is (appropriately) a small movement, but historically it may be significant. As I noted earlier, in chapter 4, there can be no revolutions from old paradigms to new ones until the new exists. It is vital, therefore, regardless of comparative strength or influence, that new, restrained models of economic life be nurtured in contemporary society. It may take a general collapse of the modern economic system to bring about the revolution in their favor within society as a whole; or, in a more optimistic scenario the change, if voluntary, might be less violent and painful. But in any event the increasing interest in local, small-scale economics is a hopeful though still mainly symbolic development. The sorts of interests that made *The Whole Earth Catalogue* such a widely bought book, that resulted in new experimentation with solar heating and windmills, and that led many to renewed discovery of the delights of home-baked bread and produce from home gardens are what I have in mind.

The principles of a homeostatic economics would renounce expectations of continuous material increase of affluence, continuous growth of economic units, continuous centralization of production. Instead, they would rest on the ideal of sufficiency, the balanced fulfillment of human need both for consumption and for a share in productive work. The technology developed by such a homeostatic economics would require an emphasis on miniaturization (for the preservation of precious material resources), on durability and repairability (to avoid the waste of obsolescence and replacement), on simplicity (to encourage the active engagement of average persons in the productive process), and quality of design (for intrinsinc aesthetic satisfaction). With such ideals, the economics as well as the politics of homeostatic restraint will be suited to the needs of the post-modern world.

II

The values of holism in the life of economics and politics are no less important than homeostasis to Polymythic Organicism. The ideal of mutuality among meaningfully differentiated parts within a larger integrating whole is compatible with (and even dependent upon) homeostatic restraint, but goes beyond it. One application of holism to capitalist society would be the development of small worker-owned and operated factories, in which the usual dichotomies between "management" and "labor" could be transcended in a higher productive intention that would allow expression in a variety of nonconventional manufacturing methods and personnel practices.

Again, holistic thinking would support the emphasis we have already noted on healthy regionalism and localism as an alternative to the radical monopolies of centralized wealth: in energy production, in banking, in food supply and processing, in transportation, and the like. The organic model commends the concept of well-differentiated parts functioning semiautonomously. To be merely dependent on others for food and energy is to be at their mercy, an undignified and sometimes dangerous position; for this reason the ideal of holistic semiautonomy would support local efforts to supplement centralized agribusiness with regional farming and home gardening, and would commend the search for energy sources to supplement the Grid.

In addition, centralization of production leads to distribution problems, with enormous lines of supply crawling back and forth across nations and across the world. Trucks rolling from point A to point B meet other trucks hurrying from point B to point A, often with items to be further processed and then expensively returned to point A again. In an energy-wealthy world (the one in which such a system was able to grow up), the vast expenditure of energy for the crisscrossing of redundant goods among market areas might make economic sense despite the waste involved. But the illusions of endless energy wealth have gone, and with them has disappeared the apparent rationality of a system that sends nearly identical products thousands of miles into each other's regions of production, to be expensively advertised there in order to promote artificial preferences for the exotic as opposed to the local variety of the same item. Holistic consciousness, allied to the need for homeostatic restraint, sees this as absurd economics in a world of increasing scarcity. Semiautonomous regions should save transportation energy and other distribution costs by keeping to local products for local consumption, so far as possible. In the long run, greater diversification within regions will be necessary for this ideal to be effective, but even at present great savings could be achieved by more emphasis on the virtues (and distinctive traditions) of localities. Not only would it make good economic sense; holistic differentiation of regions would also tend toward the dehomogenization of modern chain-store, quick-food culture.

Holism, on the other hand, could not support the excess of regionalization that might destroy the awareness and reality of larger meaningful unities. One consideration is practical: the world is simply not laid out in potentially self-sufficient regions. Even the United States, which comes as close as any large region to potential self-sufficiency due to its vast expanses of farmland coupled with great varieties of natural resources, depends heavily on imports of all kinds. World supplies of petroleum are notoriously uneven in distribution, but so also are coal supplies, water power, and even usable quantities of geothermal, wind, and solar energy. The ideal of full energy independence for all regions seems simply unrealizable; significant supplemental local energy production is feasible and advisable, certainly, but the world was not designed for self-sufficiency in energy for all regions. Likewise regarding food production, some areas are endowed by nature with vastly greater capacity than others. Regional production is advisable and important so far as possible, and deserves local support. It is sad to witness the harassment given to farmers who try to remain in production despite the pressures of urban sprawl. Instead of the punishment of tax disincentives they should be given the honor and reward due to primary producers on whom all other forms of production depend. Still, the fields of Iowa are more bountiful than the rocky hills of New England. The ideal of regional differentiation and semiautonomy should not mean that New Englanders must sup on stone soup while Iowans calculate without computers. Holism, while supporting the meaningful functioning of parts, stands for the recognition of unity transcending such parts. Precisely because the parts are not all the same, or capable of functioning in identical ways, the whole (in this case the nation) is the natural unit for facilitating mutuality and integration for the common good.

The other consideration, besides the realization of practical necessity, is moral. Trade among regions means interchange of more than goods. It also stands for the interconnectedness of human life. Sometimes this point gets lost in discussions of the importance of regional semiautonomy as an alternative to the overcentralization of economics and its absurdly wasteful consequences. Once in private conversation with E. F. Schumacher, who is (as I described earlier) giving needed leadership in the direction of economic localism, I was startled to hear him declare all trade, especially international trade, a "necessary evil." At this point I had to take issue. Trade is necessary, yes, and it is sometimes a foolish evil when it is in the service of mere economic greed and unlimited expansionism; but this is the abuse of trade, not its essence. The alternative to trade, including international trade, is parochialism of mind and surly xenophobia of spirit. With the birth of the caravans and the merchant ships of ancient days, came the pushing back of boundaries of all sorts. Enlarged consciousness of different customs, beliefs, and myths spread through the world with the traders' packs. It is probably no coincidence that the spiritual alertness of Israel, the fountainhead of three major religions, emerged at the conjunction of major trading routes through the narrow fertile crescent connecting differentiated civilizations in Egypt and Mesopotamia. It is almost certainly no coincidence that philosophy was later born at the major trading center of Miletus, poised strategically between Europe and Asia at the crossroads of the commercial world.

Trade is the economic manifestation of holism's ideal of mutual interconnection among differentiated parts. Absolute economic self-sufficiency is therefore a false pursuit, even if it were possible. This is evidently true on the national level, where regions, even though healthily differentiated and decentralized, need to complement one another for the common good. It is also no less true on the international scene, where the regions of the world require mutual integration in a cooperative economic world system. The alternative, though seemingly attractive in the short run, would be grim in its outcome, as Mihajlo Mesarovic and Eduard Pestel argue in their computerized study of the economic interactions of a regionalized world.

> *Our computer analysis indicates . . . that global cooperation offers much better conditions than conflict for all concerned.* But, no computer can predict whether man will be rational enough to follow this path; however, the computer does give rational men all the evidence they need to convince other men that the emergence of a new world system is a matter of necessity, not preference, and that that system must be built on cooperation. Cooperation is no

longer a schoolroom word suggesting an ethical but elusive mode of behavior; cooperation is a scientifically supportable, politically viable, and absolutely essential mode of behavior for the organic growth of the world system.

And cooperation, finally, requires that the people of all nations face up to an admission that may not come easy. Cooperation by definition connotes interdependence. Increasing interdependence between nations and regions must then translate as a decrease in independence. Nations cannot be interdependent without each of them giving up some of, or at least acknowledging limits to, its own independence.[5]

The outcome of holism in economics, then, would be to encourage the semiautonomy of well-differentiated localities and regions and nations, in ascending orders of meaningful wholes; but it would also, at the same time, discourage the part's supposing that it could or ought to be absolutely autonomous or independent of the whole within which it functions. This means that every part properly remains vulnerable to the well-being, or lack of well-being, of the whole to which it contributes and from which it receives. And in political terms, as Mesarovic and Pestel have pointed out, it means that the concept of national independence from the highest whole, the world economic system, is incompatible with the needs of the post-modern world. Nation-states, exactly like other meaningful parts that constitute yet larger wholes, must not delude themselves with ideas of their own absoluteness. Thus the economics of world-holism leads to holistic politics as well.

Political forms, as the Marxists rightly remind us, have a way of following economic realities. Holism in economic structure should consequently be paralled by a world political system that makes provision for meaningful, semiautonomous subsocieties (and sub-subsocieties, etc.) in a richly differentiated profusion—subsocieties that relate with healthy organic mutuality through the unifying intention of larger contexts. Those larger contexts, at the world level and at each lesser level, should not be conceived as having a monopoly of power over the parts each integrates.

Humankind has known enough of despotic rule in its history not to want another superdespotism at the level of world government. World government is obviously needed to avert world conflict; the primary context for the human intention of surviving as a species has now become planetary. Not only for the prevention of catastrophic war, but also for the facilitation of worldwide economic cooperation (equally necessary for long-term survival), world government will be of basic importance to a holistic post-modern political system. But if holism is to be preserved against potential planetary tyranny, our accustomed model of government itself needs radical reconsideration. Government needs to be not a coercive force for the imposition of a legislative or executive will to order, but an integrating lure toward meaningful levels of jointly achievable values.

I am discussing ideals, of course. In reality provision must be made for the minimization of conflict: first by accommodation of divergent aims into richer synthesis, if possible; but then, when unavoidable, by the least force necessary to preserve the fundamental intention of world government itself. The principle of holism, however, would limit coercion to the minimum required for the continued integration of basic human intentions at the world level; it would never be used to achieve good, in other words, but only to ward off harm. New good, in holistic systems, is produced by mutuality among the parts if it is attained at all. Sometimes, if the lure toward value is rejected, this may result in the loss of possible achievements, and such loss must be regretted as always serious, frequently even tragic. But holistic political coordination should be seen as a necessary condition for the creation of value through mutuality, not as the sufficient condition for imposing "good" by force. The losses may be real (though often imposed favors are less unambiguously good than the imposer sincerely supposes); still, these losses must be borne as the lesser of the evils involved. Some of the worst tyrannies in human history have begun as ardent desires to achieve great values by any means necessary. The likely outcome of conceiving world government as coercive benefactor, I fear, would be the imposition of planetary homogeneity and the destruction of real mutuality and semiautonomy for the parts that differentiate our world and preserve its cultural richness.

The same holistic principles of political structure also apply to the nations. Nations should probably survive, as valuably differentiating subunities, into the post-modern world; but during our transition basic changes in practice and concept must be accelerated. No nation should through its state apparatus have the power to impose its will on other states by unilateral coercion, much less possess the means to render the planet desolate at its whim. The concept of the state itself, if statehood entails "sovereignty" of the (now obsolete) absolute sort, needs to be abandoned. Trends toward real disarmament or weapons limitation agreements, including provisions for multilateral inspection and enforcement, are consequently to be encouraged and vastly amplified on the principles of a holistic politics. Doom by war, as we saw in chapter 1, remains a real and even likely end to all our hopes for a humane and livable post-modern world. The question whether the human race has a viable future at all, therefore, hangs on ridding the world of the immense quantities of "final" weapons that now threaten the extinction of all of us. The difficulties are probably insurmountable without widespread consciousness change. Thus, the three major principles of Polymythic Organicism all are vital for this high priority for survival. *Homeostasis,* restraint both affecting the patterns of greed that drive nations to military conflict and limiting the absolute freedom of states to wield weapons of planetary hazard, is a first prerequisite for the climate in which dismantling may begin to occur. *Holism,* a sense of mutual

interest among nations within the larger intentions of world
cooperation for survival, will make simultaneous withdrawal
from the brink a realistic policy. And *creativity,* the
inventiveness that must find solutions to the complexities of
arranging for worldwide safeguards against the rebuilding of
weapons of mass destruction, is the key to long-term safety for
whatever society the future may bring.

The dismantling, in practice and profession, of state
sovereignty is an essential step toward the recognition of real
mutuality among the nations of the earth. The same principles
apply, of course, in the establishment of binding international
economic agreements regarding currency, food, energy, and
trade. These are matters essentially of global intention; the
nations properly contribute as parts to this larger context of
integration, even as they constitute meaningful wholes for their
own populations.

On this internal national level the principles of holism in
politics would urge that government still be conceived as
minimally coercive and maximally facilitative of the healthy
fulfillment of all its parts. Such parts, of course, are defined
differently in different nations. Some are federally organized,
some have provinces, nearly all have some sort of regionally
differentiated subunits. The relationships among these parts will
differ, quite correctly, in different circumstances. What political
holism stands for, ignoring what those detailed arrangements
may be, is the presence of structures allowing for mutuality
among the regions and for genuine give and take between all
parts and their integrating national government. The important
matter is that political health depends upon constant mutual
adjustment, not one-way manipulation. What I earlier called
the "control syndrome" is a constant hazard that government
officials at every level must be required to avoid. Control itself
is not the issue; the alternative to any sort of control is chaos
(though chaos is not so close, nor so frightening, as many
overcontrolling functionaries seem to fear); the primary issue is
whether control is one-way or mutual. Healthy organismic

controls operate via internal feedback loops that allow the various parts of the organism to control each other, constantly, sensitively, and in the interest of the organism as a whole. Political health at any level depends upon the same sort of intercourse both among the parts and between the parts and the organs expressing the integrating intention of the whole.

In the last analysis, of course, the significant centers of intention, those who coordinate their activities in more and more complex orders of political expression, are people. This is not to say, reductively, that the unities we call political institutions are mere abstractions. They are not. Far from vaporous concepts only, the entities called nations (and states and regions and towns, etc.) have the power to shape and to shake. The modern world is all too familiar with the damage that can be done by nationalism run amok. But the fact remains that political entities, while *molding* and *motivating* people, are still *made up* of people and, in principle, exist to facilitate the fulfillment of human intentions. That principle, finally, is fundamental to political holism. From world government, unified around the human intention to survive as a species on the threatened planet, to the local ward, integrating human intentions to maintain street lights or to install new sewer lines, political activity is an expression of human needs and interests. It is ordinary human beings who need to be connected to local governments by intimate feedback loops in order to maintain mutual control over common activities; it is ordinary human beings for whose general benefit the various other levels of political apparatus are devised and to whose real fulfillment holistic political structures will constantly defer. In such ways, then, the holistic values of Polymythic Organicism will point toward needed avenues of reform and hope in the politics, as well as the economics, of our transition to the post-modern world.

III

The third of the principal values supported by Polymythic Organicism is grounded, we have seen, in the creative inventiveness of life. There is an interiority, a for-itselfness, a purposive power in living beings—experienced at an especially high order in healthy human persons—that confers both dignity and zest upon those who possess it. The fact of human dignity in being sentient bearers of intrinsic values and purposes is what stands, at bottom, against the manipulative approach toward people. Mutual influence and control is compatible with organismic values; but reliance on the control syndrome, the habitual recourse to one-way manipulation, tends to reduce other people to hollowed-out "manifesters of behavior," only, and to lose sight of the essence of their humanity. This is basically why the "behavioral engineering" approach to our historical situation is profoundly mistaken and dangerous. Technolatrous illusions of manipulative omnipotence are hard for many to put aside, especially when the world is in desperate need of deep reforms in how people behave. They turn, therefore, to grand schemes of manipulation (as I noted in chapter 7) through advertising and television and the churches; or they turn to coercive political tactics, many of them with a distinctly fascist flavor; or they put their trust in tinkering with market forces designed to produce the desired result.

I have no objection, as must be clear by now, to the use of some sorts of economic or political or psychological means for the facilitation of a humane transition to the post-modern civilization that must follow ours. Such means are unavoidable aspects of life and, when appropriate to the ends they seek, are quite legitimate. But the engineering approach to such means as levers for the moving about of pawns is wrong. People are not pieces standing inertly on the board of history waiting to be pushed or pulled by external forces into cleverly predetermined designs. People have designs of their own! Behavioral engineering is fundamentally wrongheaded because based on an inadequate model of human nature. The inadequacy of the model accounts for why it is that large-scale engineering of history never seems to work. Investing heavily in the one-way manipulative approach to social reform, therefore, is a mistake, in part because it is very likely to be ineffective.

It is also a mistake because, even if successful, it would contaminate the post-modern world with the same seeds of objectivistic, reductionistic determinism that we have come to see in bitter fruit today. Means must be nondestructive of their ends. Since the end is not merely survival but human survival within a flourishing natural environment, a choice of those means that enhance human dignity and enlarge the scope of human consciousness is mandated. Regimentation and manipulation express contempt for human consciousness and the powers of creative self-determinism that Polymythic Organicism seeks to nurture and expand. Therefore the means of social change must, on this strategy, be gentler, more loving and patient, than those prescribed by the well-intended but still technolatrous advocates of behavioral engineering.

In part the patience required of Polymythic Organicists is due to their respect for the multiplicity of purposes that human beings, in their inevitable differentiation from one another, may pursue even within a common context of ultimate values. Genuine pluralism demands listening and negotiating and mutual accommodation. No individual may assume that he or she has a monopoly on good intentions or on wisdom; no group may suppose that it has nothing to learn from other groups. It is true that there are limits to accommodation. Defense against the crass exploitative stance toward nature and the dominating posture toward persons is permitted by the least disruptive or alienating means available. But if organismic post-modern consciousness becomes more generally assumed as a basic framework for life through and beyond the transition, the possibilities for creative pluralism will multiply. Even now in many circles the possibilities for mutual listening and learning are hardly being realized to their fullest extent.

Another reason for loving patience is that much effective spreading of organismic values will necessarily be through symbolic actions that are themselves means appropriate to the ends pursued. New consciousness cannot be engineered; it spreads by contagion, by contact with symbols that are first seen, then felt, then lived. Here we find the paradox that symbolic acts—utterly "ineffective" in the quantitative scales of modern *realpolitik*—may subtly help to change the world.

These symbolic acts arise somehow from the inventiveness of life—its capacity to find new ways to express its own basic intentions. Against the despair we find so prevalent in many modern circles, Polymythic Organicism pits hope in this creative potential.

The acts need not be dramatic to be deep. I am thinking of such simple shifts of natural behavior as to the practice of baking bread at home, again. The feel for the grain, if it is ground at home, or the sense of the life-bearing presence of the loaf that rises—in contrast to the alienation from basic nourishment symbolized by the rows of cellophane-cocooned loaves of factory-whipped foam the modern supermart calls bread—restore a measure of simplicity to consciousness, as well as a sense of quality to the palate, that the modern world has largely lost.

Other changes in diet may be both symbolically important and potentially of practical help to the hungry world, as well. The rediscovery of meatless meals[6] (not necessarily full vegetarianism, though some may wish to go that far) releases protein and energy otherwise extravagantly lavished on those few wealthy moderns who have become accustomed to eat unprecedentedly high on the food chain. Pleasant family meals —and occasional company meals as well—with the explicit recognition of the symbolism of an ecologically less exploitative diet, may heighten awareness of the world's health as well as one's own.

Creative symbolism in transportation practices will play a part in the transition to new consciousness. Reduced thoughtless use of private petroleum-fueled transportation (including private boats and—alas—airplanes!) and increased attention to sharing rides, will combine good symbolism with prudent management of resources. I am hopeful that new attitudes and practices may spread to include the lowly hitchhiker, who serves, when picked up, to increase the efficiency of the host automobile in passenger miles-per-gallon and to decrease its per capita pollution rate. Some system of registering and identifying bona fide riders and drivers should not be too difficult to devise in order to diminish the threat of criminal abuses (both ways) that constantly haunts current hitchhiking, after which the natural presumption would be in favor of sharing a lift when space is available. Here is an area in which the homeostasis of the hiker should stimulate creativity from society in the interests of the mutuality that holism supports. Besides, sharing rides can lead to interesting conversations and broadened horizons.

More walking, as a matter of course, and more bicycling, as a matter of efficiency and pleasure, are good symbolic acts. As the practice spread, the demand for sidewalks and bicycle paths will grow. And as they are provided the real possibilities of alternative ways of getting to destinations will expand. The vicious circle of feeling unable to use one's bicycle to ride to work because of the hazards of heedless automobiles and the horrors of breathing pure exhaust fumes on the way, once broken, can lead to a salubrious circle of decreasing pollution and congestion as more and more riders leave their cars at home in favor of the green-belt bicycle paths and walkways of our transitionary cities.

Recycling practices, made part of the domestic routine, including the washing and squashing of tin and aluminum cans, the sorting and saving of bottles and paper, and the habitual purchase of returnable bottles in preference to energy-wasteful (and more costly) throwaway containers, make for good symbols of the closed circle of material transformations in which we live, willy-nilly, aware or not. The fact that "everything must go somewhere" and that "everything is connected to everything else"[7] can be simply but effectively symbolized in such ways as these. Homeostasis in the market basket and holism in the kitchen can be creatively expressed in every household where the new awareness spreads.

These are only a few examples of the symbolic expressions, in daily life, of the religious position I have called Polymythic Organicism. These are mundane, of course, in every way: this is exactly why I chose to discuss them here, toward the end of a chapter dealing with economics and politics. They are at the level of daily life, of simple citizen action, and yet they incorporate and publicly manifest the values of this candidate for post-modern religious consciousness no less well than (and perfectly compatibly with) the simple act of a Jew or a Christian in giving thanks to God before meals or in contributing towards the support of charitable works. Genuine religion insinuates itself at all levels of life, and guiding purposes illustrate the values that religion represents.

The eventual practical effectiveness of these symbolic activities, of course, depends on their ability to insinuate themselves not only into the fabric of a few private lives but also into post-modern society at large. The personal practice of them, as intrinsically right whatever the practical outcome, is profoundly important (as I have said before) if new consciousness is to take root anywhere and spread at all. But collective activity in the interest of shared values is also one of the appropriate expressions of a holistic consciousness in which individuals are vitally related to larger wholes. Here creativity and inventiveness play a major role as well, since the choice of collective methods must not be self-defeating. But the power of political association need not be merely manipulative. It can be informative and persistent as is Common Cause; it can be principled and steady as is the American Civil Liberties Union; it can be ecologically sensitive and personally oriented as are many local conservancy and consumer organizations.

The inventiveness and resiliency of human life is not to be discounted, then, as we assess our resources for the transition to the post-modern world. The times are in need of a new consciousness, one that can rejoice in the pluralistic possibilities of human differentiation even as it unites individuals and society around the basic organismic virtues of richness, wholeness, and proportion.

We have found possible support for such consciousness in religion, in education, and even within politics and economics. This does not mean that Polymythic Organicism is bound to sweep all rivals before it as the post-modern world is born. Powerful forces are arrayed against its values. But the deepest need of the post-modern world is assuredly for the values of life. And where there is life, there is hope.

Notes

1. Ivan Illich, *Tools for Conviviality,* p. 54 ff.

2. Ibid., pp. 55–56.

3. Ibid., p. 56.

4. E. F. Schumacher, *Small is Beautiful.*

5. Mihajlo Mesarovic and Eduard Pestel, *Mankind at the Turning Point: The Second Report to the Club of Rome* (New York: E. P. Dutton, 1974), p. 111.

6. *See,* for a few good examples, Frances Moore Lappé, *Diet for a Small Planet* (New York: Ballantine Books, 1975): Ellen Buchman Ewald, *Recipes for a Small Planet* (New York: Ballantine Books, 1973); Adrienne Crowhurst, *The Weed Cookbook* (New York: Lancer Books, 1972); and Catherine Lerza and Michael Jacobson, eds., *Food for People, Not for Profit* (New York: Ballantine Books, 1975).

7. Barry Commoner, *The Closing Circle,* pp. 29–41.

POSTSCRIPT ON HOPE

This book ends on a hopeful note. The whole of part 3 was a search for actual trends or possible policies worthy of hope in our time. I have no wish to apologize or recant; despair, the alternative to hope, is a profitless posture. Hopelessness is all to easy. It is passive, even destructive. The listlessness of despair is one of the burdens that those alert to the needs of our transition time ought not to be forced to bear. Hope motivates. Hope heals. Hope lures toward better things.

Hope, however, is not the same as optimism. I am not optimistic, if optimism implies a firm disposition to expect happy outcomes no matter what the evidence. Optimism, under present circumstances, is likely to be fatuous. The optimist persuades himself or herself that the better outcome is the more likely one. That this is not the case today I tried to emphasize in chapter 1. No one who is alert to the perils of our world situation can fall into the narcotic dreams of simple optimism.

The main difference between healthy hope and flabby

optimism is that while optimism comforts itself behind its rosy lenses, hope knows how to say a constructive "nevertheless" to acknowledged circumstances that tempt some to the "little suicide" of despair. Erich Fromm has said it well:

> Hope is *paradoxical*. It is neither passive waiting nor is it unrealistic forcing of circumstances that cannot occur. It is like the crouched tiger, which will jump only when the moment for jumping has come. Neither tired reformism or pseudoradical adventurism is an expression of hope. To hope means to be ready at every moment for that which is not yet born, and yet not become desperate if there is no birth in our lifetime. There is no sense in hoping for that which already exists or for that which cannot be. Those whose hope is weak settle down for comfort or for violence; those whose hope is strong see and cherish all signs of new life and are ready every moment to help the birth of that which is ready to be born.*

To hope is to affirm life as pregnant with creative possibility. Such affirmation, expressed simply and sincerely in daily tasks, is the organismic sacrament that saves the world.

*Erich Fromm, *The Revolution of Hope: Toward a Humanized Technology* (N.Y.: Harper & Row, 1968), Chapter II.

INDEX